FIT to RIDE

IN 9 WEEKS!

The Ultimate Exercise Plan:
Achieve Straightness, Suppleness
& Stamina in the Saddle

Heather Sansom

Illustrated by Marg Henderson

T S
TRAFALGAR SQUARE
North Pomfret, Vermont

First published in 2016 by
Trafalgar Square Books
North Pomfret, Vermont 05053

Disclaimer of Liability
The author and publisher shall have neither liability nor responsibility to any person or entity with respect to any loss or damage caused or alleged to be caused directly or indirectly by the information contained in this book. While the book is as accurate as the author can make it, there may be errors, omissions, and inaccuracies.

Trafalgar Square Books encourages the use of approved safety helmets in all equestrian sports and activities.

Library of Congress Cataloging-in-Publication Data
Names: Sansom, Heather.
Title: fit to ride in 9 weeks: the ultimate exercise plan: achieve straightness, suppleness & stamina in the saddle /
   Heather Sansom.
Description: North Pomfret, Vermont : Trafalgar Square Books, 2016. |
   Includes bibliographical references and index.
Identifiers: LCCN 2015031428 | ISBN 9781570767302
Subjects: LCSH: Horsemanship--Exercise. | Horsemanship--Health aspects. |
   Horsemen and horsewomen--Health and hygiene.
Classification: LCC RC1220.H67 S26 2016 | DDC 798.2--dc23 LC record available at
   http://lccn.loc.gov/2015031428

 Illustrations by Marg Henderson
Photographs by Heather Sansom and Carrie Smith
Exercise Models: Ifrah Ibrahim, Heather Sansom, Mike Van de Water
Book design by Lauryl Eddlemon
Cover design by RM Didier

Typeface: Myriad
Printed in China
10 9 8 7 6 5 4 3 2 1

This book is dedicated

first to my parents who inspired me with
a love of horses and physical movement, and
the life values of pursuing excellence and
helping others, and second to the team
of people and horses who taught and
encouraged me along the way, and
who make this work so rewarding.

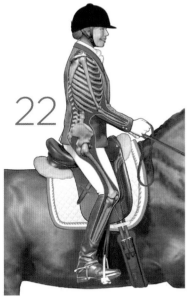

22

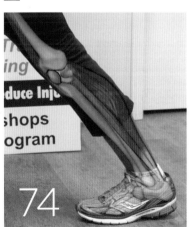

74

87

Contents

About Heather Sansom

Photo courtesy of Heather Sansom

Heather Sansom is a certified personal fitness trainer and equestrian coach through the Canadian national equestrian federation Equine Canada, as well as a Level 1 Centered Riding instructor. In the mid-2000s, she developed expertise in fitness and biomechanics for riders, leading this field in North America. In 2007, she launched her coaching business Equifitt.com and has since published over 200 articles on rider fitness in national and international equestrian magazines, as well as several books.

Heather has spoken and conducted workshops at regional, national, and international equine symposia on rider fitness and athlete development, including the Equine Canada Annual Convention and the Certified Horsemanship Association International Conference. She has provided fitness and conditioning coaching to Olympic and elite riders, and through Equifitt.com, Heather offers online personal training and riding instruction to equestrians worldwide.

Heather also provides wellness coaching and is completing her doctorate in youth resilience through equine-based physical activity. Passionate about horses for over 40 years, Heather's main personal riding focus now is classical dressage. She counts polo, mounted games, foxhunting, horse trials, competitive trail, skijoring, barrel racing, trick and liberty training, and driving among her many varied equestrian experiences.

PART I

Introduction to Rider Fitness

Why Get Fit?

Skeleton:
1. *Radius*
2. *Humerus*
3. *Scapular*
4. *Pelvis*
5. *Trocanter*
6. *Femur*
7. *Patella*
8. *Tibia*
9. *Calcanius*
10. *Tarsus*
11. *Metatarsus*
12. *Philanges*
13. *Cannon Bone*
   (Metacarpals)

Muscles:
1. *Trapezius*
2. *Deltoid*
3. *Rhomboid*
4. *Latissimus Dorsi*
5. *Superficial Gluteal*
6. *Biceps Femoris*
   (Hamstring)
7. *External Obliques*
8. *Internal Obliques*
   (Thoracic Ventral
   Serrated Muscle)
9. *Triceps Brachii*
10. *Brachial Biceps*
11. *Anterior Superficial*
    Pectoral

A

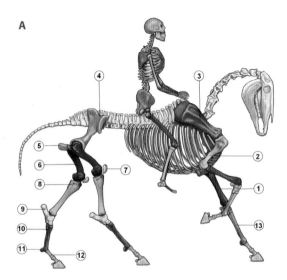

B

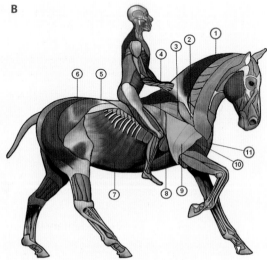

1.1 A & B Corresponding parts of human and horse
noted in color: skeleton and muscles.

●●●

The rider influences the horse in ways beyond most people's immediate perception, and the way a rider uses her body greatly impacts the way the horse is enabled or blocked from using his. The new integrated structure involves both species in a way that goes well beyond the simple application of aids by the rider and performance of actions by the horse (figs. 1.1 A & B). For example, riders with locked ankles have an impact on the freedom of movement of the corresponding joint in the horse (hock). Riders who are not engaging their core influence a similar lack of engagement in the horse through the way the two bodies interact. Similarly, riders with tense long back muscles influence a similar phenomenon in the horse.

There is no magic involved. The relationship is biomechanical. Since there are feedback loops (information receiving and sending) going in both directions (rider to horse, and horse to rider), both species can impact one another. This is why the rider's role of leadership through physical contact is so important, and why a rider who is fit for the task can ride better—and with greater resilience or prevention of injury.

Great horsemen and women in all disciplines develop a special "feel" for working with horses—whether from the ground or in the saddle—that depends on an unwritten language of body, intent, energy, emotion, and specific aids. Horses as prey animals are highly tuned to human body-language subtleties.

Most horses are willing to do whatever is asked of them, provided the human involved is fair and demonstrates safe leadership. There is an amazing range of things a horse can be trained to do: from pulling logs through a forest on voice commands, to performing any of the Olympic disciplines, to liberty work such as that seen in the show spectacular *Cavalia*. Working together with horses is a lifelong quest for harmony: professionals and amateurs alike share a common goal of achieving increasing fluidity and oneness with horses. Once bitten by the bug for this adventure, it is many people's dream to continue communicating with horses until their last breath; there is always more to learn, regardless of a rider's situation.

> *While riding is a great way to maintain an active lifestyle, riding on its own is not enough."*

Rider Fitness for All Disciplines, Bodies, Ages, and Abilities

In the years since I started my practice as a fitness and conditioning coach, I have worked with riders of all types: from elite athletes in all disciplines to keen Pony Clubbers and adult amateurs taking up the sport for the first time in their fifties or even sixties. In clinics and private practice, the riders have come with Western, endurance, jumping, dressage, and even treeless saddles—or no saddle at all. The important common element is the human body interacting with the equine one.

Regardless of the preferred riding discipline, level of expertise, training philosophy, or personal body shape, all riders do better when they take care of their bodies by doing activities outside of riding. While riding is a great way to maintain an active lifestyle, riding on its own is not enough.

The reason why so little was written about the condition of the rider in classical riding manuals was because in Europe where these manuals originated, it was taken for granted. It's only in recent decades that we've reached a place in our modern lifestyle where the tone and body awareness of the majority of the population is not maintained at a "sport-ready" level. Our lifestyle is so sedentary that most people are not carrying their best physical self into their chosen leisure activity—including riding. This is unfortunate because the horse must then make up the gap.

Since horses are so much bigger than we are and cannot speak out loud, they have to compensate for their riders' lack of physicality. If they spoke our language, they could tell us exactly how they have become stiff in one shoulder or misaligned. Evidence of this is seen in the ever-growing need for all manner of equine therapists to address lameness and straightness issues. If riders stayed off the horse's back, many of these problems would not arise: Among practitioners I have spoken with, it is quite common to note that the horse's imbalances and strain issues correspond very closely to physical patterns evidenced in his most frequent rider.

FITNESS NEEDS DIFFER BY RIDING LEVEL

In my practice, I have discovered that professionals need to pay attention to physical readiness just as much as amateurs, but for different reasons. Whereas amateurs tend to have less tone and physical awareness by virtue of their relative lack of time in saddle and physical training, professionals develop other problems from *too much* repetitive activity: they develop tensions, strains, and imbalances by virtue of riding so many horses and doing so much other farm-related work, without attending to their body fitness as if they were an athlete in training. The overall physical demand has a negative impact on longevity, effectiveness, and performance in the saddle. Still, many people erroneously assume that since they are already doing so much physical labor, more exercise is unnecessary.

In fact, serious training is even *more* critical for a professional wishing to avoid repetitive strain injury. Using horses as an analogy, let's consider how there are:

- Unfit ones.

- Not-fit-enough ones.

- Fit ones—but not for the activity they are being asked to perform.

- "Ring sour" ones that need to do something fresh and different to loosen up and get "immediate responsiveness" back in their main game.

The same classic categories can be applied to riders.

Reasons to Keep Yourself in Shape

Why rider fitness? While mindfulness and minor adjustments during riding are very important, the body that dominates your riding effectiveness is the one you carry to the saddle. A body that is not as responsive as needed gets tired and starts to "collapse" while riding, or has tension patterns that create repetitive asymmetrical strain on the horse. This body cannot magically become tuned, supple, and responsive with mindfulness exercises alone.

To create another mental picture for you, imagine learning to drive your car around an obstacle course. Now imagine that your tires are out of alignment. You can focus all you want to on the course, but you will not be able to drive it with finesse and lightness if you have to haul on the wheel sometimes to compensate for a "pull" to the left. You might also miss some cones on the course and knock them over. There would be uneven wear patterns on your tires, *especially* if you drove more and more with these misaligned wheels in the hope that more "practice makes perfect."

Everybody can easily understand from this analogy that fixing a car's misalignment—one that impacts driving it with balance and symmetry—has to be done at the garage. No amount of driving the car with increased mindfulness and focus, or new compensatory patterns of movement, will make things go better until the physical problem is fixed.

Straightness, suppleness, and *stamina* for riding are like the Holy Grail. In all disciplines, the goals are to enable your horse to understand what you ask and be physically fit to perform it, and then for you to stay out of his way so that he can move in ways his body is designed to move to perform the task. While it is certainly true that the surest way to ride better is through good riding and good riding instruction, we have achieved understanding in sport science that we must also engage in deliberate acts of self-tuning. A not-supple, not-straight, weak person does not suddenly become a straight, supple, strong rider any more than she could suddenly become such a skier.

If you are reading this book, there is a strong chance that you appreciate the topic of fitness and that you engage—or have engaged—in activities to work on yourself. All riders can benefit from a "return to basics" from time to time. Even if you are a professional rider with a regular gym workout routine, it is good to take time out in your life to reset the basics. Most horse people understand this principle because we do this with horses all the time: when something has

Compensatory Patterns of Movement

When your body does not recruit muscles in proper or efficient order, it does what it can with the patterns it knows best, even though they are less efficient. For example, you have probably seen someone with an ankle or leg injury develop an odd gait, which is retained even after the injury is supposedly healed. The reason for this is that the brain and body have reorganized themselves to accomplish movement without the correct muscle-use sequence. This is a workaround when a section of the body is briefly unusable. When a compensatory pattern continues, it wears down other areas in ways not optimal to their design. The person with the compensating gait, for example, commonly develops hip- or back-strain issues as a result of the uneven way of walking she has developed.

Vocabulary Terms

Functional fitness: Fitness that contributes directly to the way your body needs to move for some other task (as opposed to muscle-isolating exercises on machines, for example).

Integrated core: When your core-muscle engagement or training is integrated into a movement so that your body learns to use your core strength as part of your movement pattern (as opposed to isolated exercises unrelated to functional movement).

Spine stabilization: When your body has been trained to use your core muscles and posture awareness to maintain a stable spine posture that is ergonomic (useable) while you are doing other things, so healthy and correct spine usage is not compromised by movement or effort. A stable spine is also a *neutral spine* most of the time.

Neutral spine: When the spine is stabilized into a position of anatomic neutrality: it is not bent or curved in any direction. A neutral spine is associated with the *athletic-ready* position.

Athletic-ready: When the body is held in a position with a neutral spine and uncommitted to a particular direction so that you can move in any direction you need to. Riding requires constant adjustment to return to *spine neutral* or an *athletic-ready* stance (most balanced) as the body responds constantly to different directions of movement from the horse. Lack of neutrality or readiness places the body behind the horse's movement.

not been working quite right, or the horse seems to have lost his freshness, you know that it's time to take him back to revisit basics.

So, whether you have been less active than you want to be, or so active that you are on the verge of a strain injury; whether you ride once a week, or several horses seven days a week, my Fit to Ride plan will help you return to basics and do a physical "foundational reset" that will improve not only your enjoyment of your ride but also harmony with your horse.

Even if you do not ride often or even at all, this workout plan will help with self-carriage and fluidity in your body that will improve your communication with the horses you work with on the ground, as well as your enjoyment of other activities.

FITNESS AND GENDER

Since riding is all about a rider's vertical spine moving together with a horse's horizontal spine, all riders of both genders can benefit from developing the strength and suppleness needed to ride well while minimizing strain and injury to self or horse.

Although much that has been written recently on rider body-and-mind topics seems to be geared toward women, my workout is not "ladies only." The exercises chosen are selected from my years of training riders and other athletes of both genders. I specialize in *functional fitness* training and in integrated core and spine stabilization. Without the ability to move the way you were designed to—while maintaining spinal neutrality (see sidebar, p. 6), you are an injury waiting to happen.

My program contains exercises that are quite different from a non-equestrian training program because they focus on body areas and patterns that are specific to riding. Many non-equestrian training programs, especially for men, focus on strengthening the body in ways that may actually work *against* good riding.

All humans have the same core postural muscles. Riders of both genders share the same trends in tension patterns (usually based on discipline rather than gender). The Fit to Ride program is based on what is common to riding needs. The workouts apply equally to men, women, young, old, experienced, and less experienced riders, and all saddle types.

If there is a unique quality to the sport of riding, it is the requirement that riders balance their yin and yang—male and female—natural tendencies. Riding requires women to become stronger and more assertive, at the same time as it requires a toning down of the more aggressive or "male" tendency to use physical strength to achieve goals.

A beautiful golf swing and a beautiful ride have in common that neither can be achieved by force *or* passivity; instead they need a balance of strength, softness, coordination, and timing. This is what we call *suppleness*; it is also what we call the leadership-and-partnership dance between any horse and human.

I am often asked whether there are specific exercises for riders. The short answer is yes and no. Fitness that is *marketed to* riders is not the same as fitness that is *truly for* riders. Real conditioning for an activity trains the body in movements that don't seem at all like the actual activity most of the time. The reason is that joints and muscles need to be trained in their range and along their length in order to create a healthy balanced body that can perform in the sport activity.

Sometimes rider fitness means training your body with exercises that cannot be done in the saddle; if they "mimicked" riding all the time, they would merely reinforce the tightness patterns that riding develops. Other times, rider fitness means training your mind and body together to have efficient connections and movement patterns that can translate directly back into the way you move in the saddle. Some of these types of exercises often appear to mimic riding movements.

The human body moves and functions best in specific ways regardless of the sport or activity being performed. If this were not the case, physiotherapists would have to specialize in only helping people with specific recovery for specific activities. So, the best riding always turns out to be in alignment with the classical and proven understanding of how the body should move. The best riding,

> *Real conditioning for an activity trains the body in movements that don't seem at all like the actual activity most of the time."*

of course, does not always equate to the best competitive performance. We know that there are times when sport pushes athletes—human and equine—into moments when form and function become secondary to the goal or performance.

For the most part, training to ride better is largely grounded in basic classical training: a more symmetrically balanced, better moving, self-carrying, and conditioned body. Thus, a rider, just like any other athlete, is best served by doing training that promotes a full range of motion in joints, plus integrated core support for movement with suppleness (without any blockage along muscle and fascial chains).

Luckily, there are many different exercise modalities that can contribute to this requirement, making it possible for all individuals to find some activity they enjoy and stick with—probably more important than doing specific exercises, unless there is an injury or specific problem to be addressed.

Riding versus Other Sports

Because the rider rarely uses his or her body in a large range of motion, the actual need that riders have for training joints and muscles in full range is less apparent, and riders and trainers mistakenly think that since riders use small ranges of motion in riding, training for riding should only cover that small range of motion. Consequently, many riders do not get a sufficient range of motion

in movement for joint health and suppleness. As a result, they suffer from ligament shortness, muscle tightness, and joint blockage with a negative impact on pelvic and spine usage. Many strains and aches actually *result* from riding, both in amateurs not riding often, and in professionals riding for many hours daily, because the rider's body is insufficiently conditioned to manage the demand made on it from repeated, short-range motions. In the case of amateurs, the strains are more acute. In the case of professionals, the issues are usually more related to long-term wear and tear.

It is standard in serious sports conditioning to assume that the *in-game* range of motion is quite small as compared to the range needed *in training* to ensure joint mobility and stability and full-length muscle development and suppleness. Many riders are not aware of this training standard because they have not had experience with serious training in other sports. While the promotion of physical activity and fitness is helped by the availability of a lot of free information on the internet, the source is cluttered by popular notions and inaccurate ideas, and credibility is often confused by vulnerability to strong marketing. Even riders keen on fitness but unfamiliar with sports conditioning, can be exposed to many erroneous training ideas circulated in the fitness industry, or confused by the often unclear distinction between activity options and actual conditioning.

Similarly, the need for cardiovascular

stamina is more subtle than riders realize—many of them unknowingly place their hearts under undue strain at peak riding moments when they are not actually conditioned for it. Thankfully, more frequent heart attacks don't occur; however, lack of oxygen from insufficient cardiovascular conditioning still results in insufficient muscle stamina or momentary loss of precision in aids and response, both of which can place the rider at greater risk for injury. Unfortunately, lack of stamina or coordination due to insufficient cardiovascular conditioning is often erroneously identified as a lack of strength in a particular region or some other problem. Or, it is assumed that if the rider just rides more, she will accomplish cardiovascular conditioning. The level of effort needed for human cardiovascular conditioning is not something that can fairly be accomplished on the horse, since it would cause the horse to repeat more jumps or moves than he needs for his training. And it would cause the rider to make all kinds of strange weight shifts on the horse, which do nothing for respecting the guiding principle of riding: to follow the horse's movement and stay out of the horse's way while guiding him.

Riding is not ground-based—at least, not for the human. Riding is more like canoeing, luge, or acrobatics than any other sporting activity. The reason is because the base of movement for a rider is mostly *not* in the feet; it is in her seat or in a coordination of movement starting with the inner-leg connection with the horse. A casual observer who maybe has never ridden and who does not understand human and horse biomechanics—or their combination—has a very difficult time being fully able to advise a rider on conditioning. I have only run across the writings of one non-riding conditioning professional (Dr. Eckart Meyners, author of *Rider + Horse = 1* and *Rider Fitness: Body & Brain*) who has an accurate understanding of rider biomechanics.

Finally, like any other sport, riding also includes movements special to riding: it requires coordination of movement with seat, thigh, foot, hand, head, and spine, which are different in detail from movements used in any other sport. Despite the many similarities with other sports and sport conditioning, coordination of subtle movement and the need for muscle memory for accurate movement create an additional need for training neuromuscular connections in ways that are not shared with other sports. Consequently, while many exercises that are suitable for riders are shared in common with the large body of sport-conditioning exercises, it is possible to make adjustments to them that add value for a rider's unique neuromuscular coordination and muscle-memory needs.

Knowledgeable Support Is a Must

Understanding riding from the *inside* is critical for the trainer and therapist who wish to make sure their work with the rider truly aligns with riding needs. Many fitness trainers who do not ride make the mistake of thinking, for example, that posting trot is just like doing squats, and that the main source of strength is the rider's leg for powering movement from the foot.

Such a mistaken assumption can be costly for a rider if it results in the trainer's recommendation of exercises that don't help or exacerbate riding-specific weakness/tightness patterns. For example, I have met riders erroneously convinced that they needed more leg strength to squeeze the horse. Consequently, their trainer had them doing exercises that made the unproductive compensating pattern (squeezing and locking down their thighs) even worse.

Riding is more like canoeing, luge, or acrobatics than any other sporting activity."

I have seen other programs designed by non-riding trainers where they had a rider conditioning their biceps, having identified what they thought was a need for arm strength. They didn't understand that the rider's key problem was resorting to gripping tendencies, and that this particular rider needed to train her body to activate other muscles and *minimize* activation of the biceps. When I work with such a "grippy" rider, one of the first things I do is remove as many exercises involving gripping from the training program as possible. Every good fitness trainer, physiotherapist, or kinesiologist can help a rider develop more straightness and suppleness in her body, or restore proper joint function generally. However, unless they have a kinesthetic (body awareness from experience) understanding of the rider's bodily needs, they will rarely be fully accurate when prescribing exercises to address riding-specific issues.

Also, it can often happen that a practitioner's understanding of *one* discipline, does not prepare him or her to be highly accurate with a client practicing a *different* discipline. I have found, for example, that in spite of riding for several decades, I had to take polo lessons myself in order to accurately train a polo-playing client. Once I had done this, I realized that the program I had already designed for my client only covered 70 percent of his requirements. I only needed a few polo lessons to learn the movement patterns enough to adjust his program appropriately. Even as an experienced rider, I was amazed how much I had missed by never having had to swing a mallet on horseback.

I can almost tell what a fitness trainer's own riding background is, based on the types of programs they design or promote. After the common essentials are covered, there are big differences in the way a physical trainer or therapist with a hunter versus a dressage background understands body-movement requirements in the saddle. Since most riders in North America do not fully cross-train like they do in Europe, fitness trainers and body therapists who ride can often have quite wide "blind spots" in program design. Still, riders can also benefit from program elements *not* in vogue in their discipline. The reason is that fitness trainers (of whatever type) who also ride or coach riding, often tend to settle on a fitness modality (type of fitness activity, such as Pilates) that works for *them*. They naturally make the assumption that the same modality may be adequate for all other riders in their discipline. Actually, riders have individual needs based on their personal characteristics, athletic gaps, and discipline—and the time they have available. So, while Pilates may be just what one rider needs at the time, it may not be the answer for a different rider—or even that same rider at a different time.

It is very unusual for a rider to have all the time in the world to work on the many areas of her fitness that could be addressed. Usually, riders have to focus more on one area than others before switching to a different focus as their bodies condition.

In my training practice, I draw on multiple disciplines and use them as needed, depending on the individual or group. In a written program, such as this one, which is the same for everyone using it, I still draw inspiration from several training approaches. My goal in a published training plan such as Fit to Ride is always to address the common needs riders have for balance, symmetry,

suppleness, and cross-body coordination and awareness, as well as stamina, core strength, and flexibility. Since I know that different bodies, ages, genders, and riding disciplines will create an individual experience out of the workout, I build in exercise variations that riders can select from.

This Fit to Ride program incorporates the many elements just discussed, to help you build body symmetry, core strength, core stability integrated with movement, proprioception, efficient movement patterns, balance, cross-body coordination, and stamina—all of which you need as a rider. These elements have been blended together in different combinations each week so that you are continuously working on them in different ways throughout. Sometimes, they are mentioned in the *Theme* of a particular week or as a direct *Goal* of a specific exercise (see pp. 77–8 for examples). Other times, they are part of the additional benefits of a particular exercise or combination of exercises, without being specifically mentioned. While training for riders is complex, I try and keep the training program itself simple—at least in terms of what you are asked to focus on each week and with each exercise.

Like a horse, you can only physically and psychologically cope with one clear objective at a time. Trying to be conscious of too much all at once causes physical confusion, and this, in turn, makes for a reduction in safety and accuracy in both fitness training and riding.

Cross-Training and Self-Carriage

Even though there aren't any single exercise modalities that are *the* magic solution for all riders, several of them use training approaches more compatible with riding needs than others. It is helpful that there are mainstream exercise options that meet needs for rider's bodies, because that makes it much easier to cobble together a weekly or monthly exercise pattern in which the elements contribute different parts to riding needs.

Cross-training for riders is like cross-training for horses: the goal is not to be excellent in the cross-training activity but to have variety from the main riding discipline. Even riders can become "ring sour" physically. Variety keeps coordination and responsiveness tuned, in addition to providing the necessary muscle and ligament range of motion and usage previously described.

Pilates and martial arts are good cross-training modalities for riders because they are systems that presume a body-coordinating movement in space rather than from the ground, thus initiating movement from the *core* rather than the limbs. Also, both incorporate complete *movement chains* (see

> *Cross-training for riders is like cross-training for horses: the goal is not to be excellent in the cross-training activity but to have variety from the main riding discipline."*

sidebar, above) with engagement through the core and train the body in ways that are quite different from any other ground-based, sport-training approach.

Centered body control is the basis of self-carriage. The negative effects of lack of control over "loose ballast" when your body is moved by the horse are significant. This does not mean that a rider cannot have body fat, but it does mean that self-carriage and an ability to make minute responsive adjustments are critically important.

GROUND-BASED TRAINING

Technically, the combined biomechanics of horse and rider are ultimately ground-based. All the motion that a rider responds to and works with comes from the impulsion generated from the horse's contact with the ground. Joining a horse and rider together creates an entirely new biodynamic for both species where the rider is *not* ground-based, even when he or she is in a jumping position with legs quite short and standing firmly over the stirrups.

The horse also has to rebalance himself constantly (to self-carry). It is easy to understand the mutual impact of self-carriage if, for example, you compare the difference between a child riding piggy-back on you and two circus performers who carry each other seemingly effortlessly through a routine on a swinging bar or hanging ribbon, or even a figure skater lifting a partner (figs 1.2 A & B). Imagine if you were to carry the child on your back across a log over a swirling river or through an obstacle course, how you would quickly discover the need for combined self-carriage (involving quietness, balance, coordination, and harmonization between your weight-center and the child's.)

Riders Are Unique People

It is important to remember when reviewing some rider-exercise materials, that just because a photo shows a fitness model in riding clothes—and in a position that looks like she might be when on a horse—it does not necessarily make the exercise valuable for a rider. With all your training choices, be aware of how an exercise, modality, or program will contribute to your personal needs. Riders not only have different needs at different times based on discipline and personal goals, but also

1.2 A & B Circus performers show us how precise self-carriage through a common center of gravity needs to be (A). Imagine you are your horse. Have you ever thought how hard it is to carry another person piggyback if he or she is not balanced and centered (B)?

●●●

based on individual physical deficiencies. To be very brief, just as with training horses, not all riders need to use all the tools in the box. Also, not all tools are suitable all of the time. You change over time. Your training program should, too.

I have explained how individual a rider's training plans need to be; it is also important to understand that there is a '"base" common to all riders. For many years, I have referred to a "Rider Fitness Training Scale," which I see as very similar to the Dressage Training Scale, and which I explain in depth in Chapter 2 (fig. 1.3).

When training a horse, there are common basic skills and physical abilities needed before his training can advance. Quite often, a rider will get a new horse that has moved along well but still has a noticeable need to revisit some basics before he can proceed further in his training. This is because if he were to just go on, he would develop compensating mechanisms that become problematic in the long term. As we've said, humans are no different.

Many successful professional riders are really brilliant, but their success does not necessarily mean they are free of compensatory movement patterns that can put them at risk for repetitive strain injuries or be a factor in preventing them from performing to their desired level. Anyone of any riding ability, experience, age, or gender can benefit from revisiting and reinforcing the foundational basics. Also, just as with horses, the human body and brain benefit from taking time out to do something a little different.

HITTING THE RESET BUTTON

My program, Fit to Ride, works on foundational basics and can be done alongside other activities you may already be enjoying, as long as you have the time to do so. Other riders may not have time to add something new. I suggest that to get different results, it can be beneficial to pause the fitness activity you normally do, and try this Fit to Ride program. When you go back to your other activity, you may find that you have even more ability for it because you have taken time out to work your body in new ways, increasing your *physical vocabulary*.

Changing up what you are doing from time to time can also help you get out of a rut. I have found that riders will gravitate to favorite fitness activities or sports outside of riding that they are comfortable with, and which play to their strengths. Sometimes, as in the case of the many riders I know who run, this activity can be creating tension patterns that work *against* riding, even though running

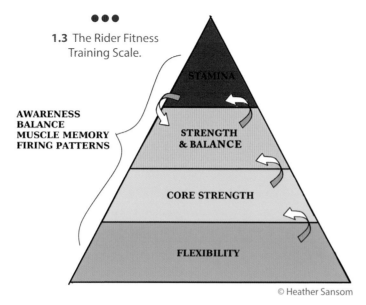

1.3 The Rider Fitness Training Scale.

AWARENESS
BALANCE
MUSCLE MEMORY
FIRING PATTERNS

STAMINA

STRENGTH & BALANCE

CORE STRENGTH

FLEXIBILITY

© Heather Sansom

also contributes other good fitness elements.

Taking a little break can help work out any of those tension patterns, allowing the rider to start fresh with a more balanced body. Also, training in a way that is a little different might push you to work on things that don't come naturally to you. It may feel awkward at times, and you may be tempted to skip steps. Many times, I find riders with a problem avoid fixing it. An example is really tight hamstrings. It takes discipline to stretch an area that you do not usually stretch so many people avoid doing it.

The benefit of doing a termed program such as Fit to Ride is that you know you are signing on for a set number of weeks and that you are free to do whatever you want to afterward. Knowing that you are committing for a specific time period can help you try something new and stick with it as an experiment.

It is possible that you may experience various emotions when you encounter exercises where you do not feel very proficient. Carry on with them anyway. It is not how perfectly you do the program but the act of taking your body through the process that will effect positive change. Think of a weight-loss program: it is possible to hate the process when following it and to not be perfect at it. Yet, most success with weight loss has more to do with sticking with it than the actual program. Good feelings will come at the end when you see how the process has helped retrain your body in areas that were holding you back in your riding.

You do not have to look like the models in the exercise photos. Just trying a new exercise to the best of *your* ability has benefits. The important element in all the exercises in the Fit to Ride program is how you are engaging the muscles involved, not whether your morphology (human conformation) or fitness allows you to look just like the picture, especially if trying to do so would compromise the muscle usage intended.

PART II

Training the Rider's Body

chapter 2

Good Training Is About
Building Balance

Riding requires the human body to be flexible (staying with the horse's movement and not blocking his motion); be strong with stamina (maintaining tone and an ability to direct the horse, as well as avoiding fatigue, which can make you more susceptible to an accident) and be well-coordinated (both consciously and unconsciously). If you simply follow the motion of the horse, you will just be an inert passenger—not a rider. So, in addition to balancing and rebalancing your own body despite movement introduced by the horse, you must also use your body proactively to direct and rebalance the horse. And this applies to every discipline (figs. 2.1 A & B).

As mentioned earlier, the Rider Fitness Training Scale is a lot like the Dressage Training Scale (see fig. 1.3, p. 14). There is a priority as to what must be achieved before it makes sense to move forward to the next stage. However, as you progress, the *first stages* must be maintained or training will be compromised. While other riding disciplines may not have a visual training model quite like the Training Scale, nearly all trainers are aware of a similar concept within their own discipline. As with training horses, it is important to understand the purpose and direction of the overall picture of training before getting lost in the details of specific muscles and exercises.

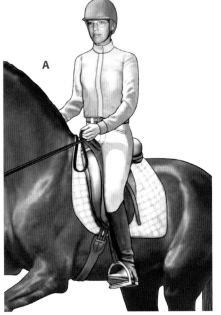

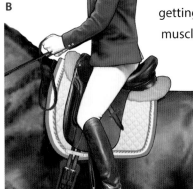

●●●

2.1 A & B Balanced rider positions in dressage, from a three-quarter and side view.

Rider Fitness Training Scale Foundation

ELEMENT 1: FLEXIBILITY

The first element in the Rider Fitness Training Scale is *flexibility* of the joints, which requires supple muscles. All human sport requires a preliminary condition that the body not be blocked in its ability for movement. Unless you have looseness and flexibility in the joints, you cannot make adjustments without introducing negative tension to your body.

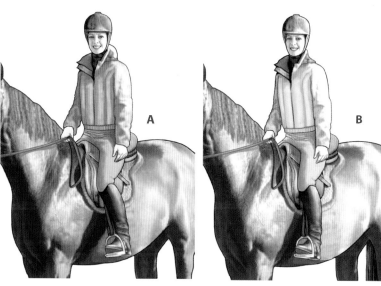

2.2 A & B A balanced hunt seat rider (A) and a rider with tight hip flexors (*psoas*), causing a "chair-seat" position with the leg forward of the desired line (B).

● ● ●

Hip Flexors *(Psoas)*

Tension affects hip mobility and rider position. A very simple example is a rider who has a tendency for her legs to shift forward into a "chair seat" due to tight hip flexor muscles (figs. 2.2 A & B). Tight hip flexors (*psoas* muscles) cause a rider's leg to creep forward and her lower back to hollow. When she tries to correct it, she fights the tight muscles by applying strength with other muscles in order to shift her leg back and keep it there, but she increases the tension in her body. This tension reduces motion in the hip even further. It can have other effects as well, such as strain on the lower back.

It would be much easier for a rider to shift her leg back if she did not have to fight the

About "Neutral"

Anatomically Neutral

This is the phrase used to describe the view of a body from the front without contraction of muscles. For example, it is like a body lying on a table with arms and legs slightly falling open away from the torso as if the person were asleep or completely relaxed.

Spine Neutrality

This is the term describing the correct position of the spine, where it is neither roached nor collapsed, so all the joints in the vertebrae are capable of full and proper motion. The spine can be neutral in upright, horizontal, or other positions, depending on the degree of bend at the hips. It can also be *non-neutral* in all these positions when the spine's natural curve is compromised.

resistance created by a tight opposing muscle. Muscles and ligaments cross over the joints. When they are tight or knotted, they lock down the joints and limit movement. No amount of mindfulness can undo the physical fact that is a shortened ligament or knotted muscle.

Tight hip flexors are a common problem, partly due to our seated modern lifestyle. In the illustrations here, various hip flexor muscles are shown that need to be stretched to allow you to get and maintain a good leg position while avoiding tension.

The drawings at the top of this page show the hip flexors (*psoas*) in an *anatomically*

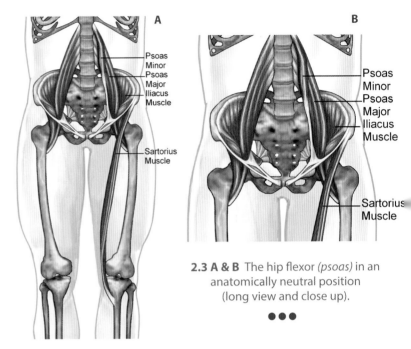

2.3 A & B The hip flexor *(psoas)* in an anatomically neutral position (long view and close up).

●●●

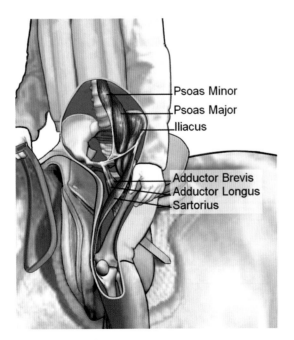

neutral position (figs. 2.3 A & B). The drawing below shows where the tight muscles are on the rider (fig. 2.4). When the hip flexors are tight, they pull your lower back forward, thus compromising *spine neutrality*. The resulting hollow in the lower back can cause back pain since your spine cannot properly absorb the horse's movement when the vertebrae are not free to move as they should. Some riders go for back massage to treat pain instead of treating the cause—the tight hip flexors, which also pull your legs forward, making good leg position difficult to maintain without tension.

●●●

2.4 The hip flexors *(psoas)* in the tight "chair seat" riding position.

ELEMENT 2: CORE STRENGTH

Once you have developed the habit of getting more flexible and maintaining joint mobility, the second foundational piece in rider fitness is strength in your core muscles. These muscles are more than just the *abdominals* (muscles on the front of the stomach on the outer layer) that people commonly think about.

The *rectus abdominis* is the abdominal muscle on the front and outside of the stomach area commonly referred to as a "six-pack" or "eight-pack" depending on fitness level (fig. 2.5). It connects at the pubic bone and bottom of the sternum, and is responsible for both curling—and resistance to curling—the body forward.

Riders who curl forward or slouch may have a shortened muscle, or simply an unconditioned one. A strong *rectus abdominis*, like a strong support post in a house's basement, prevents the collapse of the rib cage forward. Exercising this muscle at its full length is important. Many people's understanding of what core muscles are is limited to these stomach muscles. However, the core is a system of torso-area and torso-connected muscles supporting posture.

From a skeletal or hard structure point of view, the rider's waist is extremely vulnerable to excessive motion (figs. 2.6 A–D). When you look at the skeleton, a very small section of spine is all the structural support a rider has for the 4-inch area between the bottom rib

and pelvis. There are also 24 joints in the spine that sit on top of the horse and experience waves of motion from their base. Core muscles wrap around the torso in layers, and go in different directions to create an effect something like the cables on a suspension bridge. The multi-layers and multi-directions of the various muscles support torso stability and movement. Training the core involves so much more than simply doing some crunches or exercises for the frontal *rectus abdominis*. (In the next chapter I discuss other core muscles—see p. 27.)

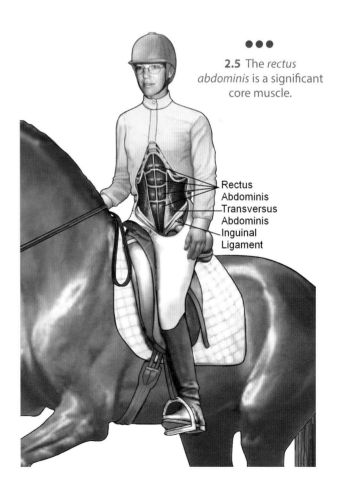

● ● ●

2.5 The *rectus abdominis* is a significant core muscle.

Rectus Abdominis
Transversus Abdominis
Inguinal Ligament

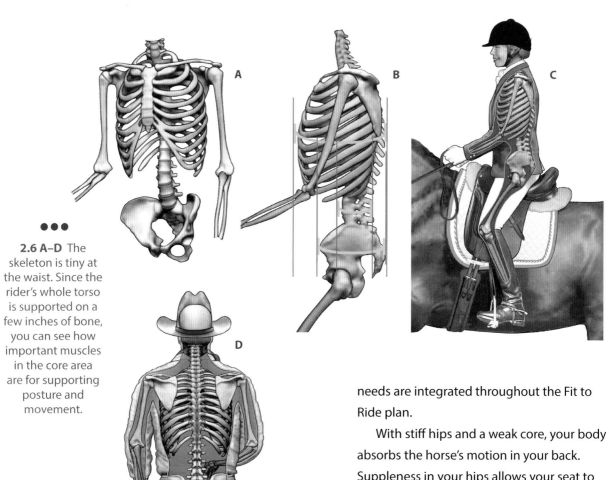

2.6 A–D The skeleton is tiny at the waist. Since the rider's whole torso is supported on a few inches of bone, you can see how important muscles in the core area are for supporting posture and movement.

needs are integrated throughout the Fit to Ride plan.

With stiff hips and a weak core, your body absorbs the horse's motion in your back. Suppleness in your hips allows your seat to follow the horse instead of transferring the motion to the unprotected and hyper-mobile lower back. Having strong muscles in the core means that any excess motion can be managed through these muscles, instead of through the spine and hip joints. This is because muscle (soft tissue) is designed to respond to motion in ways that ligaments and bones are not.

When the force of motion is effectively captured through strong core muscles, they can control the appropriate movement of your hips and spine. When it is not, the hips and spine can experience excessive strain. Also, when core muscles are not strong, the

Core Strength Supports the Back and Controls the Aids

Without good core strength and stability, a rider's back is unprotected and subject to wear and tear. Many riders with back pain would do well to exercise their mid and lower abdominal area as well, and work on hip flexibility. Many exercises addressing these hips and spine ligaments naturally tighten up as your body's way of providing joint support. Unfortunately, for a person who wants to be physically active or ride, the joints are also locked by this body response, making activity (including riding) a source of negative strain.

In addition to supporting a stable upper body, core strength also controls aids. Because your base is not really your feet, movement originates in and is controlled through your core. Balance, leg aids, weight shifts, torso rotation (shoulder turns), and even arm strength are all supported (or limited by) the level of a rider's core strength. Sometimes male riders with weak core strength overcompensate with upper body strength in ways that are just not physically possible for most females. Women tend to accumulate tension and tightness in their upper body and hips when their core is weak.

Riding through the core allows you to be clear, without using force—for example, being able to resist a horse's attempt to run away without actually pulling on the horse's mouth. Really good core strength that is built through movement on a variety of planes, and integrated into limb movement, enables a rider to ride initially from her torso, and secondly from her limbs.

It also enables you to be better able to apply an aid or respond to a situation on one side of the body, while keeping the other side neutral (free of tension or contraction). Good cross-coordination and body multi-tasking are made easier when both sides of your body can anchor through a strong core

instead of having to balance off each other or off the horse. Well-trained horses barely need a lower leg or hand aid because the rider has successfully achieved integration between the horse's movement (from his own core) and the rider's shifts of weight.

Horses naturally listen to a rider's weight and torso direction before they listen to hand or leg. Many problems that riders have with understanding why their horses are not listening to a leg or hand aid stem from the fact that their limb aids are not in synchronicity with torso position, body control, or weight distribution. Common problems that occur when riders are not conscious that their weight is communicating inaccurately include the horse's haunches or shoulders falling in or out and lack of bend. The illustrations on the following page show the impact on the horse of the rider's position (figs. 2.7 A–D).

ELEMENT 3: STRENGTH AND BALANCE

The next elements of the Rider Fitness Training Scale: *strength and balance* and *stamina* (see p. 25) must be built on the two foundational elements of *flexibility* and *core strength* just discussed. Practically speaking, any training program I have developed for a client mixes all the elements together. However, week-to-week progression is founded on ensuring a solid base of core strength and flexibility before moving forward. The reason is that while it may not

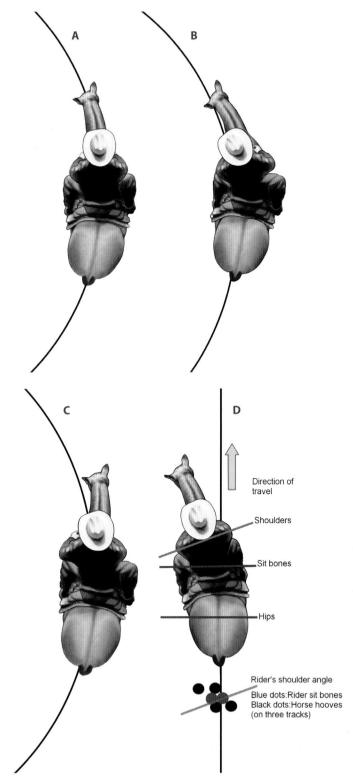

A

B

C

D

Direction of travel

Shoulders

Sit bones

Hips

Rider's shoulder angle

Blue dots:Rider sit bones
Black dots:Horse hooves
(on three tracks)

be so exciting, the rider who rushes forward to do more interesting exercises is likely to *worsen* her weaknesses. Without a strong and engaged core, all movement is compromised; there is little value in doing impressive-looking exercises with a misaligned body.

Once a rider has developed sufficient flexibility to permit good alignment and sufficient core strength to control movement, she is prepared for exercises in *strength and balance*. With proper alignment and core engagement, such exercises will reinforce all the good training that has occurred so far, and adding a weight or balance challenge will not compromise the rider's joints or smaller supporting muscles.

Without this foundation, even the best strength and balance exercises can become a source for potential strain or injury. When the rider's body is prepared and she has developed more awareness, strength exercises can be used to start building specific areas and increasing muscle mass.

Female riders should not be worried about increasing muscle. As long as the program they are using is not for bodybuilders, they will be very unlikely to overdo. The simple fact is that a large percentage of women in general, and women who ride in particular, do not develop sufficient muscle for supporting joints or promoting bone mass or metabolism. Riders

● ● ●

2.7 A–D A rider on circle with correct torso alignment (A); with a collapsed shoulder and horse popping his shoulder out (B); with only his head turned and horse pointing out of the circle (C); and in correct mirroring alignment with his horse for the shoulder-in (D).

are among the least likely to cross-train, which means that women who ride are not only more at risk for injury due to the size of horses and the height while sitting on them, but they might also have lower bone density and muscle ratio than is optimal for their age group. Middle-aged riders naturally lose muscle with age unless exercising to maintain muscle mass. As I've explained, muscle is incredibly important to support the skeleton and joints. Also, muscle size is needed in order to have stamina.

ELEMENT 4: STAMINA

Riding is a sport that requires riders' bodies to repeat relatively small movements over time. Sometimes this means a lot of time if several horses are being ridden. For safety, as well as satisfaction of good riding, the rider needs to stay alert physically. She needs to have good muscle tone and responsiveness, whether it is the first five minutes of the first ride, or the last five minutes at the end of the day.

Even riders who do most of their training in a groomed arena (as opposed to an endurance trail or cross-country course) need stamina. Stamina is trained by increasing the training time of an exercise or a workout. However, it is dangerous to do so without the proper base of good alignment, core tone that helps the body move better, and strength that supports joints. Without all the previous levels of the Rider Fitness Training Scale, the rider trying to train stamina is risking a potential injury.

Training longer and longer wears a body down and does not make it stronger when there is insufficient strength. Most people understand this principle with horses and so do not make a young horse work for too long. Or, they may use gymnastic exercises to build strength, without repeating the exercises so often they become wearing to the horse.

The exercises in the Fit to Ride program incorporate the ideas of this Rider Fitness Training Scale into the progression of exercises within each workout, and the progression of exercises from week to week. By respecting the order of the workout weeks, riders will be more able to correct imbalances and address foundational issues before moving forward to the next level.

Common Training Errors

Misalignment or insufficient core support means that lifting weights or making powerful or fast movements threatens the health of the spine or other joints. This is due to the body experiencing loading at higher intensity but not ergonomically. For example, I sometimes have clients do shoulder work with weights to recover from or prevent the possibility of rotator cuff injuries either through riding, horse handling, or other farm tasks, like lifting a heavy saddle, and repetitive motion, like stall cleaning.

However, the client is not ready for the shoulder exercises when she is still lacking range of motion in the shoulder socket (needed for flexibility), core strength, or the knowledge of and ability to maintain spine neutrality while in motion or while multi-tasking. She can do the shoulder exercises (having identified a legitimate need to strengthen the shoulder), but she does them by all manner of adjustments to her body position to compensate for the impinged shoulders. The result of these compensations is negative strain to her lower back and a reinforced muscle memory of shoulder tension. So, she cannot do the shoulder exercises until she is able to do them *without* such compensations on a proper foundation, permitting correct body alignment.

Other common errors in training are for a rider who is enthusiastic about fitness to use too much weight too early, to do too much before her body has the capacity for correct ergonomics, and to neglect the need to undo tensions created by other activities that impact negatively on riding. An example of the latter is the rider who runs regularly, but forgets to manage the tightness that commonly accumulates in the hamstrings from running.

Ironically, the keener you are for fitness activities other than riding, the more likely it is that you may be doing things that are counterproductive to your riding. It is still better to be as fit as you can be and to bring that fit body to your ride. However, attention, accuracy, and alignment of these activities to your riding goals are important.

To use another analogy, asking your body to move on to the *form* of an exercise without correct *functioning* is similar to asking a horse that is too green or unfit to do advanced movements or jump a lot. Just because the horse can get through the movement, doesn't mean he is doing anything good for his long-term performance. In fact, premature training of movements starts to lay down incorrect muscle memory that can be a real challenge to undo later.

Any rider or trainer with experience has worked with a horse that someone tried to train through shortcuts, and knows how much easier it is to build things right step by step than it is to undo faulty understanding and movement patterns. With riders, we all want to be riding as long as we can, so it is important to train with the whole picture and the long-term benefit in mind.

It is very important to understand that core strength is needed not only for movement, but also for being *still*: without strength or tone in muscles, the body acts like a palm tree or grass in the wind whenever motion is introduced. Strong muscles prevent every jarring motion of the horse from causing a rippling reaction through your torso. Since the horse moves his body through multiple planes of movement (in many directions), stimulating loading (pressure) on the rider's body from many different angles, his torso stability is much more complex than most people realize. It is maintained by many muscles responsible for movement in many directions. These will be discussed in the next chapter.

chapter 3

The Important
Core Muscles

Although the *rectus abdominis* is one of the most well-known of the core muscles (which is why I used it in explanation of core training earlier—p. 21), it is not actually the most foundational core muscle. The *rectus abdominis* is an outer-layer muscle, which you don't start with when training the core. You start with the deep inner-layer muscles that support the spine.

Deep Inner Core Muscles: *Multifidi* and *Transverse Abdominis*

Multifidi

One of the deepest muscle layers is the *multifidus* (figs. 3.1 A & B). Technically, it is a group of tiny muscles, and therefore, often referred to in the plural: *multifidi*. These small muscles connect between vertebrae at various angles, controlling both motion and the stopping of motion. *Multifidi*, weak and subject to sudden extreme loading (for example, a bucking horse) or long-term strain (such as excessive motion in the rider's waist while sitting the trot), have difficulty supporting the spine at the deepest level.

Strengthening weak multifidi is not accomplished in the same way as strengthening the larger-movement core muscles such as the *rectus*

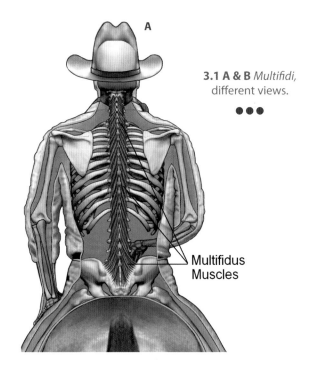

A

3.1 A & B *Multifidi, different views.*

● ● ●

Multifidus Muscles

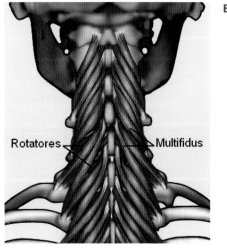

B

Rotatores

Multifidus

abdominis previously discussed. These smaller, deeper inner-layer muscles are strengthened more effectively through small movements or exercises using a held position (*isometric exercise*). In these exercises, loading (or resistance) is experienced over time through challenging the muscles to support the spine by keeping it neutral—despite weight or movement pressure to lose its neutral position.

In the courses I have taught to people recovering from back injury, I emphasize slow and incremental change with many *isometric* exercises in which the effort is more about *holding* the position rather than moving in and out of it. An example is the Plank (p. 95), which is in contrast to the *dynamic* exercises such as sit-ups that most people are familiar with (and which I don't actually use in my fitness plan because it can put negative pressure on the lower back).

The deep spine-supporting muscles of many riders may have already experienced quite a bit of negative cumulative strain, and even professionals have had incidents that compromised a vertebral disk or two. In either of these situations, it's important to take time with isometric exercises to get to the deep inner layer of your structural supporting muscles. My workout plan includes many exercises designed to stimulate the deep inner-core support muscles. Some of these, like the Plank, are specifically focused on these muscles, and others incorporate this element while focusing on another movement or other muscle combination.

Transverse Abdominis

As you work from the deepest muscles outward, the *transverse abdominis* is a critical muscle in the next layer (figs. 3.2 A & B). Think of it as a ring around your waist or a natural girdle. When I see riders using a manmade waist brace, it is often because their *transverse abdominis* is weak.

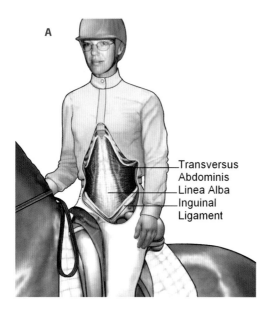

A

Transversus Abdominis
Linea Alba
Inguinal Ligament

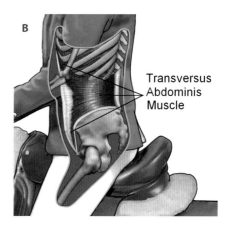

B

Transversus Abdominis Muscle

3.2 A & B *Transverse abdominis* (your natural girdle): three-quarter view (A); and from the side (B).

● ● ●

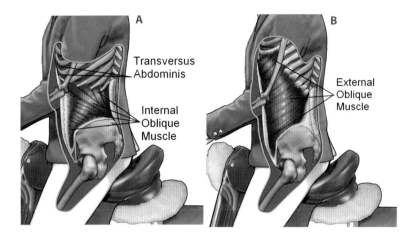

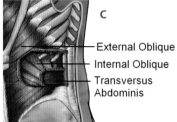

3.3 A–C *Oblique muscles* are in several layers criss-crossing your midsection like an elastic-reinforced, fabric corset: internal *obliques* (A); external *obliques* (B); showing the layers (C).

●●●

Outer Layer Core Muscles

Obliques, Erector Spinae, Gluteals, and Rectus Abdominis

Moving from the inner layers, the more visible outward core muscles include the *rectus abdominis* previously shown, *obliques, erector spinae,* and the base support complex, which includes your *lower back fascia* and *gluteals.*

Various *oblique* muscles, or muscles on your sides, are responsible for lateral and rotational movement, as well as resistance to movement, such as staying stable when your horse moves (figs. 3.3 A–C). These muscles control your use of shoulders and seat, and

Using a Waist Brace

Using a brace if you have to in order to prevent injury, or at a medical professional's request as you recover from injury, is good. Using it to replace your weak core, however, is *not* good. Depending on a brace in place of strengthening your own body (*transverse abdominis*) is like using a wheelchair when you don't need to. It would cause atrophy and even further weaken the problem area.

When you are prescribed a brace, I suggest that you use it with the Fit to Ride plan, but also discuss a plan to phase it out with your doctor or physiotherapist. A brace is a temporary fix that can become an impediment to training unless there is a clear medical reason why you cannot give it up. It acts on a rider's body similarly to the way training gimmicks can pull a horse into the right position while compromising correct usage of his body, at the same time undermining long-term development and healthy body movement. Even if for medical reasons you cannot avoid always wearing the brace, building strength in your mid-section will still improve your life and reduce your risk of injury.

your ability to align your shoulders and seat or to purposefully use them differently.

The *erector spinae* muscles contribute to controlling upright posture in seated riding and correct back position in forward-seat riding (fig. 3.4).

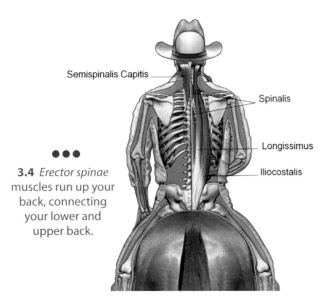

● ● ●

3.4 *Erector spinae* muscles run up your back, connecting your lower and upper back.

Even though you do not leap, jump, or run while in the saddle, the *gluteus maximus,* an important muscle for leg-powered movement, also supports correct back and leg position and usage in all riding disciplines. Your back and legs can only be as strong as your *gluteal* strength will allow, because your leg muscles and back muscles anchor in the hip area (figs. 3.5 A & B).

Additionally, the *gluteus medius* and *minimus* contribute to correct leg usage and position, as well as shoulder position, by balancing the inner-thigh muscles and providing an anchor on each side for torso movement.

Torso Control and Alignment

Obliques

In previous illustrations, *alignment* is seen in the picture of the horse bending on a circle (see figs. 2.7 A–D, p. 24). Both the horse's hips and shoulders, and the rider's hips and shoulders, turn the circle to the same degree of rotation. Otherwise, the horse is said to have his hips or shoulder "pop" out or in, or the rider can be seen to be hand-steering due to lack of

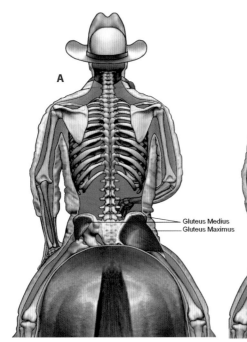

● ● ●

3.5 A & B *Gluteus maximus* and *medius* (A); *gluteus medius* and *minimus* (B).

effective use of the thighs controlled by a solid hip position (fig. 3.6).

In the illustration of a correct shoulder-in (lateral movement) on the bottom of this page, the rider's hips and shoulders are deliberately set at different rotational angles to communicate the desired placement of the horse's hips and shoulders (fig. 3. 7). Namely, hips go forward, while shoulders move as if turning a circle to create the three-track movement. From the point of view of the rider's body, the rider engages *oblique* muscles in both a shoulder-in and when riding a good circle, where the main effort of the *obliques* is to resist misalignment, or to bring the hips with the shoulders—or the shoulders with the hips. A very stable rider may look like she is not doing much when in fact she is making constant micro-adjustments to keep directing the horse to stay "straight" (that is, straight/aligned bend) around the circle. In the shoulder-in, the main work of the *obliques* is to attain a difference of positioning, maintain it throughout the movement, then return to neutral alignment of shoulders and hips.

The *obliques* also act in upright support of the shoulders. In some riding disciplines—for example, polo, roping and ranch work, or mounted games—it is necessary to drop or raise a shoulder to achieve a specific function of the upper body. In such movements, the *obliques* are employed in moving the torso. In other disciplines—such as jumping, dressage, or Western pleasure—the shoulder girdle is supposed to remain level, even when

3.6 A rider with a collapsed torso is "telling" the horse to pop out his shoulder with incorrect weight aids.

● ● ●

turning. In these situations, the *obliques* are more involved in maintaining position (or resisting movement) than initiating movement.

The *obliques* can control rotation but also contraction between hip and shoulder. Another example where *obliques* are at work is in simpler movements like gait transitions. In an up transition to canter, the rider's *obliques* must contract on one side so the rider can raise her hip and seat bone. Ideally, the horse will mirror the *obliques'* contraction as they lift into the canter lead. When a rider has trouble controlling the use of her own *obliques*, this impedes the horse from properly using his. (As mentioned, equine body workers frequently notice that horses mirror shortness, tension, or lack of activation in similar muscles to their most frequent riders.)

Weak *obliques* are quite common unless exercises are specifically done to strengthen them. Riders are not alone in largely ignoring their *obliques*. Many non-riders pay no attention to this area as well, due to the fact that most of our movement is in the frontal plane (forward and back)—or, at least, most of our conscious

● ● ●

3.7 A rider able to execute a shoulder-in with correct use of the hips and shoulders.

movement is. We know that horses have to have symmetrical lateral strength in order to move forward with true straightness, but often forget that fact also applies to our own bodies.

Perhaps the most obvious and common issue that is related to a rider's attention (or lack of attention) to her *obliques* is visible when she appears to drop one shoulder all the time. Viewed from behind, this rider has a bit of a curve in her spine. In practice, the dropping of the shoulder corresponds to difference in seat pressure. A trainer or rider will often also notice a corresponding asymmetry in the horse's ability for bend (impacted by the rider's asymmetrical weight distribution). Usually, the signs of asymmetry

Being an Athlete

Winning medals, earning money from the sport, going to expensive or elite competitions, competing regularly, hiring an expensive coach, buying an expensive horse, wearing the right gear, or maintaining an extreme training schedule are not things that make a person an athlete. The base level that makes a person an athlete is focused, disciplined, and regular practice of a sport. Athletes train "off-field" or "out-of-game" so that when they are "in-game" or in the moment that matters to them (on the horse, doing the movements), their bodies respond the way they need them to. Being an athlete is as simple as your mindset and habits. I like to say "When you train your inner athlete, eventually that athlete shows up on the outside."

that the rider is most aware of are that she cannot bend the horse as satisfactorily in one direction as the other, she has a tendency to ride more dominantly with one hand than the other, or she has a feeling that one leg is longer than the other. The feeling of one leg being longer comes from the asymmetrical seat position, but riders, especially amateurs, usually identify such feelings in a limb rather than the torso (where the asymmetry actually originates).

The rider's *obliques* are short on one side from the habitual collapsing of that side. It is almost always true that a rider who "curves" to one side has a tendency to sit in a chair collapsed to that same side. So in case there is some confusion about the rider's direction of collapse due to an asymmetry in the horse himself, it can be tested by observing the rider sitting on a chair. The curve is usually visible in postural analysis both seated and standing, in particular when the person is tired and starts to revert to her "unconscious" true posture.

When I am working with riders in a clinic, I don't always make decisions about biomechanic and posture issues right away, because early in the ride they are trying to hold themselves as perfectly as possible. If they are aware of an issue, they often have countering tension or compensating patterns that introduce rigidity into their body as they attempt to make themselves straighter or more even.

Just as when assessing the horse's knowledge, it is easier to see what the rider's true habits are when she begins to tire or reaches an exercise that challenges her enough so she shifts concentration to what she is doing, allowing her body to operate in its habitual patterns. As when working a horse, I try and get a student to relax by giving her things to do that take her mind off her own body, since we cannot do corrective or awareness work with tension, nor can she properly feel the horse. The horse is usually a very reliable teacher of asymmetry in the rider.

It is a good idea for many riders to start by stretching their *obliques* on *both* sides before a ride so that training is possible without "pull/counter-pull" tensions. Since riders develop idiosyncratic body sense of what "straight" is (due to collapse becoming "normal" to their proprioceptive senses), straightening the torso requires time and patience as the rider retrains her body to recognize and maintain true straight.

As mentioned, the torso position is not the only part of the rider impacted by shortened or asymmetrically developed *oblique* muscles. Riders can also have a feeling that one leg is longer or have slightly different ways of holding their leg position on each side. Because shortened *obliques* throw weight distribution off and frequently offset the pelvis, riders with shortened *obliques* sometimes present themselves as having a weak leg aid on one side.

Shortened *obliques* reduce the distance between the rider's shoulder and pelvis, creating what a coach or other rider will commonly notice as a little lean or curve to that side. Sometimes the lean is only in the

Body Language: Loud and Clear (But Not Always What You Thought You Said)

Our primary language with horses is kinesthetic, which means that horses "read" everything through the body. What you do with yours will speak to them. Humans make differences between intent and spoken language and this lack of authenticity causes a lot of relationship problems. Many people who are autistic or victims of abuse cannot process such differences well. In horse language, lack of "conversation" between your core and your limbs is like saying two different things to another person with your body and your voice. By and large, most horses are willing and eager to please: they do not play the disingenuous mental games that people play. If you have to nag, scold, or "talk" to your horse with your hands and legs as if you were shouting, it's likely there is a lack of conversation between what your torso and subconscious body engagement is communicating and what you think you want.

shoulders, but usually it is in the pelvis as well, which lifts one seat bone up somewhat and tilts the pelvis a little. This seat-bone lifting and pelvis tilting offsets the position of the legs. They cannot hang straight or symmetrically with an offset pelvis.

In addition to lateral drops of a shoulder or leg asymmetry, rotational biases are also commonly seen. A "rotational-tension" pattern causes a rider's shoulder to fall back, as well as drop. This makes it difficult for a rider to align her shoulders and hips, or properly guide the horse's shoulders and hips without increased use of her hands and lower legs. Rotational patterns are more complex than the discussion in this book, but it is sufficient to note that they involve the *obliques*, so training these muscles through recommended stretches and core work will help to reduce these problems.

The goal of training is *not* to give the rider more things to consciously think about doing while in the saddle. It is to *reduce* the number of conscious corrections and adjustments so the rider can focus on the ride.

The Back Is Anchored in the Hips

In classical riding it is known that everything begins with the pelvis. From the point of view of core strength, a stable, straight, and strong pelvis is needed both as a base for the spine going upward and as an anchor for all the muscles controlling movement upward and downward. Leg aids can only be as strong and accurate as the pelvis is stable. Torso position can only be as aligned as the stability of the pelvis will allow.

Working outward in the layers of core muscles controlling both pelvis and spinal position, you find the *gluteus maximus* and

The Neutral Pelvis

Like the spine, the rider's pelvis is ideally maintained in neutrality. This does not mean it stays in a fixed position, but rather that no matter what the rider uses an aid to do or how the horse's position impacts the rider, the pelvis and seat need to constantly return to a "neutral" position. This is a position that is not committed to any particular direction or weight distribution, so that the rider can shift instantly in any direction that she needs to go.

A *neutral, seated pelvis* will be upright so that the rider's seat bones are free to follow the horse's motion. A *neutral, raised-seat pelvis* will be symmetrical, without any dropping or twisting, so that the rider's weight distribution

in both legs is even and the legs can respond with the horse's motion instead of getting behind, ahead, or unevenly weighting the horse to one side.

For riders with physically different leg lengths, it is more important to adjust the stirrups to ensure a stable pelvis than to make the leg lengths appear the same at the feet. Physical leg length asymmetry should be verified by a medical professional. Many riders think they have leg length difference when what they actually have is asymmetrical muscle tension making the legs *appear* to be different lengths. A chiropractor or osteopath is generally trained in assessing true leg length differences versus false ones.

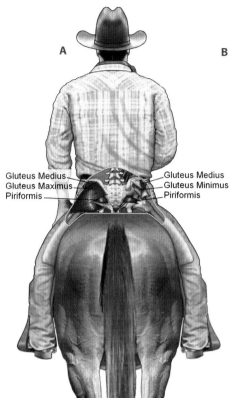

A

Gluteus Medius
Gluteus Maximus
Piriformis

Gluteus Medius
Gluteus Minimus
Piriformis

B

Gluteus
Medius
Gluteus
Maximus
Piriformis

Gluteus
Medius
Gluteus
Minimus
Piriformis

3.8 A & B
Gluteals and
piriformis.

● ● ●

medius (figs. 3.8 A & B) and the *erector spinae* (see fig. 3.4, p. 30).

Gluteals

The large muscle on your seat, the *gluteus maximus*, is a primary muscle responsible for powering human movement. It needs to be strong and powerful for nearly all sports because you cannot run or transfer energy or motion up through your body without strong "glutes." It is common for exercise trainers who are not riders to think that posting is just the same as performing squats, lunges, or pliés, and that the engine of the motion is in the rider's leg and seat as it would be for all other similar looking movements. In actuality, the energy from posting only partially comes from the rider's legs and hips. The rest comes from the momentum of the horse transferred to the rider through inner leg contact.

For a rider, *gluteal* strength is important, but not for the reasons often supposed. The strength in the *gluteals* is not for powering motion so much as it is for first, supporting rising-seat postures, and second, anchoring back positioning muscles, as well as controlling leg-aid strength. Unfortunately, most riders spend a great deal of their day sitting, which causes this large and important muscle to atrophy. Also, since riding itself is a more or less seated activity, riding does not condition the muscle sufficiently.

Many riders have weak "glutes" accompanied by tight and short hip flexors. The combined problem creates a chair-seat leg, and when the rider tries to correct the chair seat by force, it creates a locked-down hip due to muscle tension. It also makes it difficult for the rider to hold her spine neutral when the *hip flexors* (*psoas* and *iliacus* muscle), pulling on the lower back, and weak glutes provide no counter-support. They can result

THE RIDER'S LEG "BACKLINE"

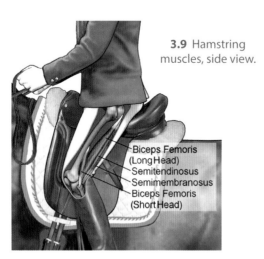

3.9 Hamstring muscles, side view.

Biceps Femoris (Long Head)
Semitendinosus
Semimembranosus
Biceps Femoris (Short Head)

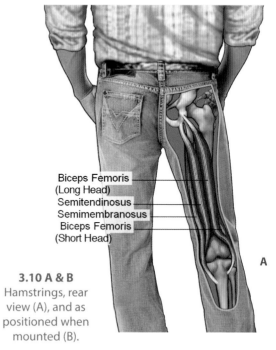

Biceps Femoris (Long Head)
Semitendinosus
Semimembranosus
Biceps Femoris (Short Head)

A

3.10 A & B Hamstrings, rear view (A), and as positioned when mounted (B).

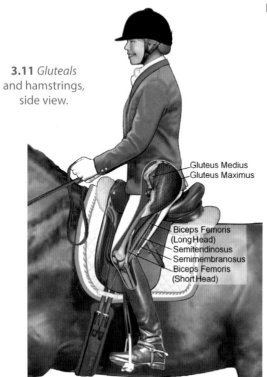

3.11 *Gluteals and hamstrings, side view.*

Gluteus Medius
Gluteus Maximus

Biceps Femoris (Long Head)
Semitendinosus
Semimembranosus
Biceps Femoris (Short Head)

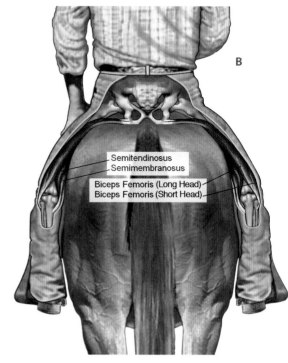

B

Semitendinosus
Semimembranosus
Biceps Femoris (Long Head)
Biceps Femoris (Short Head)

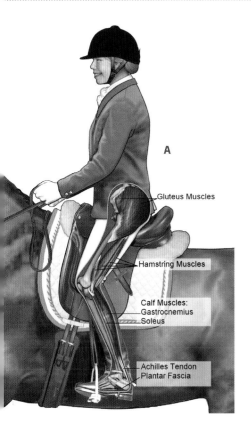

A

Gluteus Muscles

Hamstring Muscles

Calf Muscles:
Gastrocnemius
Soleus

Achilles Tendon
Plantar Fascia

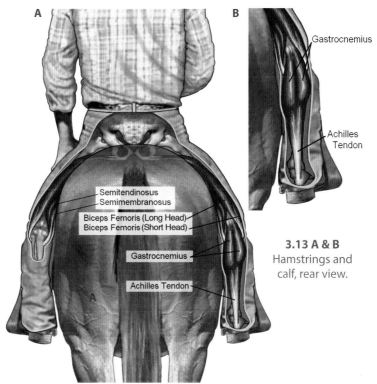

A

Semitendinosus
Semimembranosus
Biceps Femoris (Long Head)
Biceps Femoris (Short Head)

Gastrocnemius

Achilles Tendon

B

Gastrocnemius

Achilles Tendon

3.13 A & B
Hamstrings and
calf, rear view.

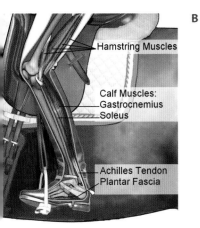

B

Hamstring Muscles

Calf Muscles:
Gastrocnemius
Soleus

Achilles Tendon
Plantar Fascia

3.12 A & B *Gluteals,* hamstrings,
and calf line, side view.

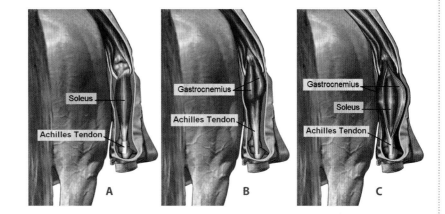

Soleus

Achilles Tendon

A

Gastrocnemius

Achilles Tendon

B

Gastrocnemius

Soleus

Achilles Tendon

C

3.14 A–C Calf muscles: *soleus* (A), *gastrocnemius* (B),
split *gastrocnemius* (C).

in a rider's inability to hold a correct jumping position over time, to have a tendency to collapse onto the horse's forehand, and to be unable to control the posting-trot action. The *gluteus maximus* is included as a core muscle because without tone in this area, the rider's hips cannot be supple and straight, and the torso has no base of support.

Erector Spinae

The *erector spinae* (see fig. 3.4, p. 30) functions similarly to the *rectus abdominis* (see fig. 2.5, p. 21), but on the rider's back. These muscles correspond to the large, long back muscles that you sit on either side of the horse's spine. They are engaged when you lift your back or hold yourself upright. These are *movement muscles*.

In horse sports involving a bent, rotating, or active back (roping, mounted games, polo, jumping), these muscles are very hard at work supporting your posture against gravity and force. In upright-seat riding such as dressage or Western pleasure, they are not used for significant movement, but they are still critically important in holding an erect posture without tension. Training these muscles for symmetry is really helpful. The *erector spinae* muscles, however, have to anchor near the pelvis complex. Think of them as a trunk of a tree, with the *gluteals* being the roots that form a base to keep the tree upright.

The Rider's "Backline"

In addition to the back and *gluteal* muscles, a rider's "backline" includes the major muscles on the back of the leg (the *gluteus maximus, hamstring,* and *calf muscles*—see sidebar, pp. 36–7). Due to our seated lifestyle, these muscles are often undeveloped, causing them to be short and tight, which has a negative impact on the rider's position and her ability to have tension-free, full body usage.

Many exercises that train the *gluteus maximus* also often train the hamstring muscle. I like riders to use bodyweight exercises such as lunges because they train proper folding at the hips and use of the hamstrings along their length (as well as the *gluteals*). Although popular in fitness gyms, exercises using machines or equipment to target the hamstrings alone are often not as useful for riders or others training for application to movement because they do not train the hamstrings functionally. In some cases, they train just one small segment of the muscle, which creates a "bunchy" muscle that is not ideal for riders.

Generally, I don't recommend exercises for riders that create "bunchy" muscles since these can cause issue with proper seat and leg position, as well as with proper body usage in the saddle. A rider can be quite strong—and should be if she also does farm work since strength training protects joints from strain. But bulky or unevenly developed muscles, especially in the legs, get in the way of the

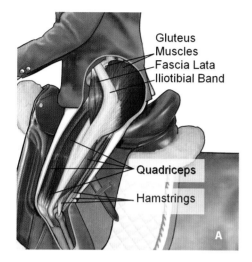

Gluteus
Muscles
Fascia Lata
Iliotibial Band

Quadriceps

Hamstrings

A

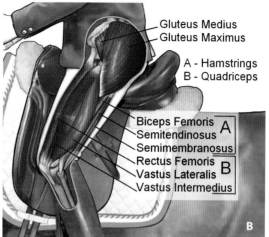

Gluteus Medius
Gluteus Maximus

A - Hamstrings
B - Quadriceps

Biceps Femoris
Semitendinosus
Semimembranosus
Rectus Femoris
Vastus Lateralis
Vastus Intermedius

A

B

B

3. 15 A & B
Gluteals and
hamstrings in
balance with the
quadriceps.

● ● ●

rider and also don't engage efficiently.

I do not recommend that most riders do exercises like leg presses (lying backward on a machine and pushing great amounts of weight with your feet), for example, because the weight loading can far exceed the rider's bodyweight. Besides creating a risk of hip injury, this type of exercise creates bulk, which again, is not functionally useful, and may even impede a nice leg position. The only application I can see for creating this kind of bulk and power might be when part of the rider's job is to leap off and on the moving horse, and she has to manage velocity and gravity in bursts without injuring leg joints (vaulting or trick riding, for example).

The hamstring is used in most human movement to bend the knee. Paradoxically, for riders, a strong hamstring helps *lengthen* the rider's leg because it permits correct use of seat and upper thigh. A weak hamstring results in legs that go into a chair-seat position, or ones that do a lot of heel-hiking

(raising the heel back to make a leg aid). Weak hamstrings can also trigger tightness in the hips because of shortness in the muscle that prevents the rider from having correctly folding hips (figs. 3.15 A & B).

In riders, strength in the hamstrings supports correct pelvic posture, correct leg aids, stamina in holding a jumping position or other raised posture (such as might be needed at certain times in polo or mounted games), and use of the upper thigh to initiate leg aids instead of nagging at the horse with the heels and ankles only. Hamstring-strengthening exercises also better balance the leg overall, helping to address any problems the rider might have with tightened hip flexors.

I have already discussed the *psoas* muscles that form part of the hip-flexor complex (see p.19). Some of the quadriceps muscles also have a hip-flexion function since they cross the hip joint, contributing to the raising of the leg. As noted, most bodyweight exercises that strengthen hamstrings also

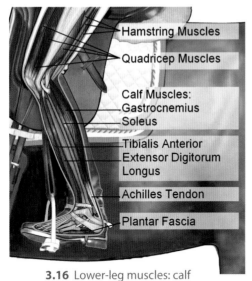

3.16 Lower-leg muscles: calf and *anterior tibialis*.

● ● ●

strengthen the hips (various *gluteals*). They often also work to strengthen the *quadriceps*, thus creating better balance. This Fit to Ride program includes many such exercises.

Similarly, riders also need balance on the lower leg between the calf (often too tight) and *anterior tibialis*, which is often quite weak (fig. 3.16).

The Lower Body and Torso Support

The *gluteus medius* is included because of its role in lateral stability of the hips, providing a base of support for leg aids on the opposite side and for leg neutrality on the same side. Also, there is a line of structural counter-support connection between the *gluteus medius* and the rider's shoulder on the opposite side, as well as the *gluteus medius* and the rider's *adductors* (muscles on the

inside of the upper leg) on the opposite side (figs. 3.17 A & B).

Because this chain crosses the sacroiliac (SI) joint, *gluteus medius* strength, which is even on both sides, helps to support the rider's low back and SI area. Many riders with a sense that they are weak in applying leg aids think that their *adductor* muscles must be weak. In most cases, people's *adductor* muscles are actually too strong in comparison with their counter-balancing muscles. The *adductors* are often unbalanced (too strong) in relation to the muscles on the outer thigh and leg, which are anchored at the *gluteus medius*. This means that the fix for weak legs is often the *opposite* of common thinking: riders with weak leg aids often need to strengthen the *outside* of their legs and hips, *not* the inside.

LOWER BODY IMBALANCE

You now know that people generally have tightness on the inside of their thighs and weakness on the outside, unless they are doing training to change this imbalance. Many people who *only* ride—without doing any other exercises—develop even *more* imbalance, especially when they are intent on acquiring increased ability to squeeze inward with the thighs (they are riding around exacerbating the problem that alerted them to an assumed need for leg strength). I have worked with several older, professional riders who, over time, actually wore down their hip joints prematurely due to a lifetime habit of *not* cross-training.

The fitness trainer who does not know about riding can make the mistake of giving a rider exercises to further strengthen already imbalanced *adductors*. This error comes from a lack of understanding the functional movement chain (described on p. 40 in the text about crossing-support lines) and the need for the rider to constantly counter-balance or counter-anchor from one side to the other so that she doesn't grip the horse to accomplish her goals. As mentioned, what is experienced as weakness in squeezing the horse, is often *not* weakness on the inside of the leg, but weakness in the *gluteus medius* and muscles on the outside of the *opposite* leg, thus preventing the rider from giving clear leg aids. It can also be related to lack of a neutral spine or pelvis (see pp. 19 and 34), which creates loss of core stability, which blocks or interrupts the body from effective movement and counterbalance from one side to the other.

Upper Body

Now that I have discussed the *lower* body—the *base of support* for the upper body—I'll return to the problems that can occur with the *upper* body. They can only really be corrected once the base of support is balanced.

Upper-body tension in our culture is quite common thanks to our constant use of computers and the general tendency for carrying tension in the shoulder area. People are also very "handy" in the sense that one of the first "go-to" actions of our brain

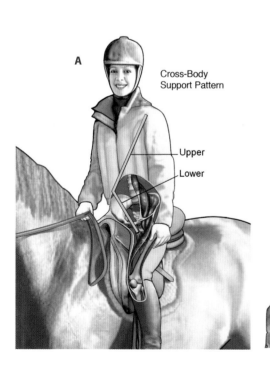

A Cross-Body Support Pattern

— Upper

— Lower

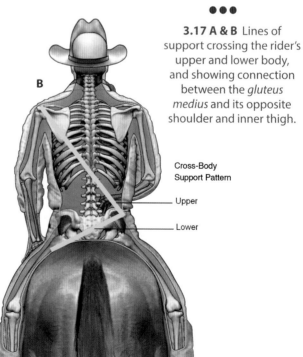

● ● ●

3.17 A & B Lines of support crossing the rider's upper and lower body, and showing connection between the *gluteus medius* and its opposite shoulder and inner thigh.

B

Cross-Body Support Pattern

— Upper

— Lower

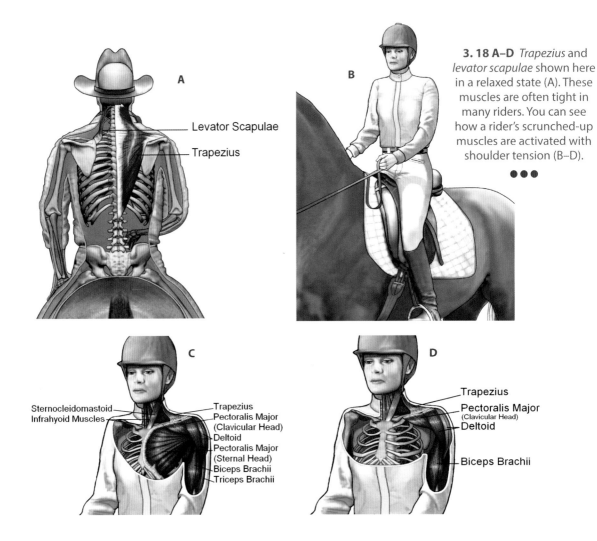

A

Levator Scapulae

Trapezius

B

3. 18 A–D *Trapezius* and *levator scapulae* shown here in a relaxed state (A). These muscles are often tight in many riders. You can see how a rider's scrunched-up muscles are activated with shoulder tension (B–D).

●●●

C

Sternocleidomastoid
Infrahyoid Muscles

Trapezius
Pectoralis Major
(Clavicular Head)
Deltoid
Pectoralis Major
(Sternal Head)
Biceps Brachii
Triceps Brachii

D

Trapezius
Pectoralis Major
(Clavicular Head)
Deltoid

Biceps Brachii

under demand is to clench or use our hands. There are biomechanical consequences: the *trapezius* muscle tends to fire (activate) very rapidly, and it accumulates tension.

THE UPPER BACK: THE TRAPEZIUS TAKEOVER

Many riders have neck and shoulder tension, which derives from the body's reaction of "turning on" the *trapezius* muscle in their daily life. When there is a neuromuscular "highway"

to an unproductive area such as the *trapezius*, there will be an almost automatic physical reaction, collecting tension in that area, regardless of what the rider is trying to do: the brain signal goes right past other less-used areas and triggers tonality in the area with the most frequent use, despite the rider's desire *not* to be tense in that area (figs. 3.18 A–D).

In many cases, reducing tension in the *trapezius* and shoulder area involves extensive stretching and retraining of the brain to use different muscles that will bring the rider's shoulders down and back.

Shoving tense shoulders back during a ride only creates more tension. In addition to the naturally tense areas, exertion used to "fight" the tense muscle area creates additional tension. The answer is not to fight the muscle that is involuntarily tense, but use its "off" switch, which is found by training the body to make better use of other areas.

There are many shoulder-strengthening exercises in the body of general fitness training that I avoid using until a rider is quite advanced in her ability to isolate various shoulder-area muscles while keeping the *trapezius* relaxed. Otherwise, she will begin the exercise with good intentions (of *not* using the *trapezius*), but the brain takes over and immediately employs its well-worn habit of triggering the *trapezius* muscle to engage. When this happens, the result is reinforcement of the negative pattern. A rider with shoulder-tension problems should be very selective about the fitness programs that she uses—including otherwise fun and wonderful fitness classes at her gym—until she has successfully trained her body to stop allowing the *trapezius* muscle to be dominant. General fitness programs often use exercises that employ the *trapezius* directly or indirectly, because the goal of general fitness is to have shoulders that are viewed as looking good when they are muscled.

The exercises in this book are selected and organized with this problem in mind, since it is so common among riders.

THE UPPER FRONT: CHEST AND ARMS

Other upper-body muscles that tend to have a "superhighway" for neuromuscular connection, and ones that tend to hold tension, are the *pectorals* and *biceps*. When *pectoral* muscles are tight, or in an imbalance of strength with their counterbalancing muscles on the rider's back, the rider's shoulders are pulled forward. This is very unhelpful because then the rider must force her shoulders back, creating upper-body general tension and blocking correct movement of the spine.

Moreover, throwing the shoulders back will force the lower leg forward. The rider will either be out of balance and behind the horse's movement with a chair seat, or she will force her lower leg back into position and also have locked hips. In either case, she is likely to experience excessive motion in the waist and consequent lower-back pain, if not vertebral damage.

Often, correct positioning is affected as well. Some riders with tight *pectorals* and "rolling-forward" shoulders tend to lean back in both riding and other exercises in order to create a sense that the top of their shoulders are level. The problem is that neutrality in the spine is completely lost. Upper-body muscle

> *The answer is not to fight the muscle that is involuntarily tense, but use its "off" switch, which is found by training the body to make better use of other areas.*

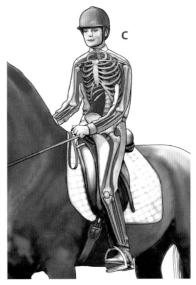

3.19 A–D Rider collapsing forward (A) and attempting to correct forward slouch with back tension, resulting in arms that are too long and rigid (B). Then, a view of her skeletal position and muscles that are shortened and tight when slouched (C & D).

● ● ●

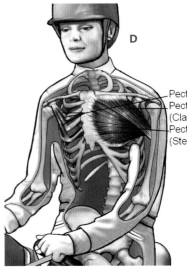

Pectoralis Minor
Pectoralis Major (Clavicular Head)
Pectoralis Major (Sternal Head)

dominance often includes the tendency to overuse the *biceps* when managing the reins. A rider with tight *trapezius* or tight *pectoral* muscles is out of balance, whether she collapses forward or forces herself back, so there is a corresponding tendency to balance through the reins by gripping them (figs. 3.19. A–D).

When a rider has been made conscious of her tendency to grip the reins (employing the *biceps*) and is trying to stop doing so, she will often go in the other direction and have an excessively loose hold on the reins out of a desire not to be hard on the horse's mouth. For disciplines that require steady contact, loose contact is just as bad for the horse as gripping since it results in intermittent contact. A sensitive horse will become anxious

or maybe take to grabbing the bit away from the rider. A kind and steady one will just become hard in the mouth and stiff in the body and neck.

It takes some retraining to reprogram a rider's body to make better use of her backline upper-body muscles instead of allowing the default dominance of the front area muscles. The backline upper-body muscles include those on the back, and the *triceps* on the back of the arms (figs. 3.20 A–C). When there is better physical mechanical balance through softness in the front and shoulders, and counterbalancing supportive tone in the back and back of arms, the rider has a much better chance of having neutral posture and using her body without automatic creation of tension in the wrong places.

Fixing Tension Areas

Making muscle areas that carry tension more supple and relaxed is only half the equation in achieving a more consistently neutral upper body. First, it involves training the muscles that have become weak and less toned as a result of infrequent stimulus; then it's about teaching the brain to trigger tonality in different muscles, instead of the ones that carry tension.

One way to think about the retraining is to liken it to teaching vocabulary. To get the brain to use other "words" (pathways to different muscles), it has to learn them. Otherwise, the brain always resorts to the "words" (muscles) it knows best, especially when under tension.

Increasing your neuromuscular vocabulary of response involves activities that also build strength. By building strength through exercises targeting the balancing muscles, you are also wiring or widening the pathway of response to that area. By practicing new muscle-engagement patterns on the ground, you increase the probability of your body

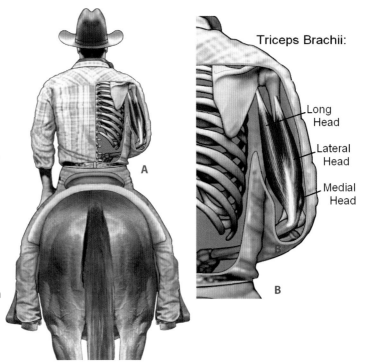

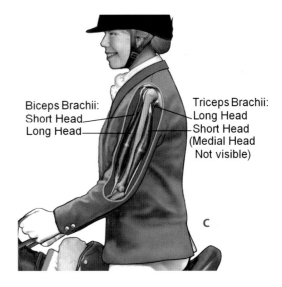

3.20 A–C Balanced arm position showing the *triceps*, rear view (A & B), and *triceps* strength in a supple rider with a relaxed arm (C).

● ● ●

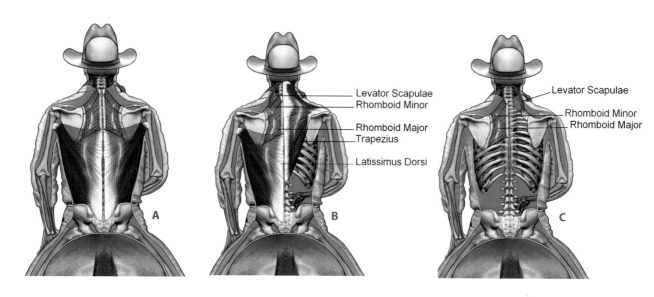

3.21 A–C Three views of the *latissimus dorsi*, *rhomboids, levator scapulae,* and *trapezius*: lats and *rhomboids* (A); lats, *rhomboids, trapezius, levator scapulae* (B); *rhomboids* and *levator scapulae* (C).

• • •

using those new patterns automatically while you are busy focusing on riding tasks. Without strengthening the balancing muscles, the suppleness attained in stretching will be lost as the body continues to revert to using its "favorite" muscles under stress (that is, loading or demand).

STRENGTHENING THE CORRECT BACK MUSCLES

Latissimus Dorsi and Rhomboids

To bring the shoulder blades back and down, allowing the rib cage to lift, thus permitting a truly neutral, "ready" posture with a lowered center of gravity and a neutral spine, it is important to train the *latissimus dorsi* ("lats") and the *rhomboids* (figs. 3.21 A–C). These muscles draw the shoulder blades back (*rhomboids*), and down (lats).

The lats also help to shorten the rider's back and support a neutral lower-back or pelvis position since they attach at the lower

back in the same area some of the hip flexor muscles attach. Most people who do not deliberately train the *rhomboids* and lats are weak in those areas and prone to tightness in the front part of the torso due to the fact that most manual labor and riding tasks happen in front of the body. Women are especially prone to weakness in these muscles.

A very common mistake made by riders with upper-back pain is to obtain therapy to further relax and soften the muscles in their back that are already weak and overstrained by being pulled forward by over-dominant *pectoral* muscles. Since the pain is in the back, the rider and therapist often think that the solution is to alleviate the pain through massage or other treatment.

In fact, such an approach makes the imbalance worse. A very good therapist will identify the tight *pectorals* and weak *rhomboids* and lats, and work to release tension in the *pectorals* while recommending exercises for the back. Similarly, a savvy therapist will identify tight *hip flexors* and weak mid-section or *gluteal* muscles and treat the cause (imbalance) rather than leap to conclusions and treat the symptoms (low back pain). Chronic pain or therapy for an area is a sure sign that the rider needs to commit to regular stretching and strengthening exercises for a more permanent solution. While important in some moments, therapy does not replace the work the rider must do in the first place to build and obtain balance.

One of the worst habits I have seen in riding that contributes to increasing tension in the *trapezius* and *pectorals* (in both horse and rider), is the use of "human side reins" where the rider sticks her arms down and out to the side to bring the horse's head down. This practice pulls on the wrong muscles in both horse and rider, creating strength under the horse's neck and resistance at the withers, while increasing tension in the rider's neck and shoulders. If the rider is a small female,

chronic riding in this way creates problems in the shoulders and neck area, which can be quite serious, particularly when the rider is a professional and works several horses, several hours a week, in this way.

The shoulder girdle is not meant to manage this type of repeated strain. I have worked with one well-known elite professional trainer who had this training technique—and the consequent shoulder-strain issues. Most amateurs do not spend enough time in this position to create an enormous physical problem, but the practice still stimulates the wrong muscle areas in both horse and rider for neutral, supple, and proper self-carriage.

Since it is not possible or advisable to do the pulling exercises needed for building strength in the too-often neglected lats and *rhomboids* while sitting on your horse holding the reins, it is necessary to do them unmounted with sufficient resistance and range of motion. There are several exercises in the Fit to Ride program to develop awareness, isolate movement, and progressively build strength in the lats and *rhomboids*.

chapter 4

The Difference Between
Riding Disciplines

The concept of the Rider Fitness Training Scale (p. 14) means that there are some commonalities in training needs for all riders. Many of these have just been discussed in the previous chapter.

Yet as mentioned, each rider's personal training needs will have differences based on personal development, strengths, and weaknesses. In addition, the rider's overall plan will be shaped by the needs of her riding discipline. I find that designing a fitness program for a rider is more about prioritizing than it is about doing absolutely everything that would be ideal to do.

When training horses, you can't do everything at once. You need to pick a couple of areas to focus on—and expect the areas of focus to change somewhat as training evolves. Yet there must always be an overall understanding of the job the rider's body needs to do.

Training for the rider's body is both *preparation* for tasks it needs to do, as well as *prevention* of injuries that could occur (fig. 4.1). We have already discussed many strain-type injuries that riders can get. Some task and injury-prevention considerations must also include non-riding time. A rider who does barn chores or other athletic tasks needs to train for those as well, so that any injury or muscle imbalance developed in those activities does not impede her riding.

To keep it really simple, I like to classify riding disciplines

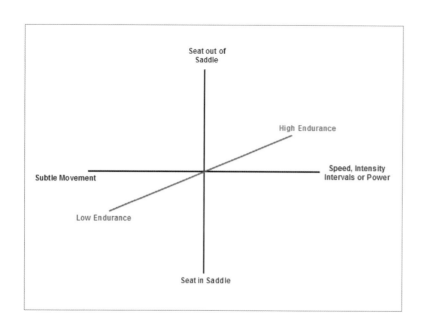

● ● ●

4.1 The key areas covered by a fitness training program.

according to the main type of seat position required, and then according to incidence of ballistic ("burst" moments, for example, in cattle roping) or interval intensity (length of sustained high effort, like a cross-country course), and level of endurance.

The way I organize disciplines for the purpose of physical training is into the following categories based on the type of demand on the rider's body: *Intense*, *Raised Seat*, and *Seated*. From the perspective of what is required of the human body, this works better than dividing training needs by saddle type. For example, an eventer and a roper have more in common in terms of training needs for high-intensity interval bursts, rotational control, and cardiovascular capacity than an eventer and a hunter rider (or roper and Western pleasure rider) have in common, even though sharing a common saddle type. In other ways, even though there are clear equipment and discipline differences, the training for an eventer and a polo player is similar due to long periods of standing out of stirrups combined with frequent changes in plane of movement, direction, speed, and load.

There are some general rules of thumb for different discipline training needs. The higher the endurance requirement, the more a rider needs to train with cardiovascular gains and core strength in mind. The more intervals of intensity, the more the rider needs to train for power-burst ability with the equivalent ability for changes from activity to stabilization and

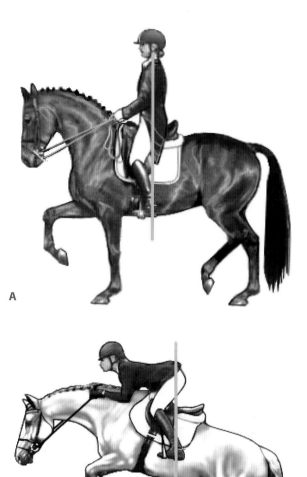

A

B

4.2 A & B Good posture alignment in the seated and raised-seat positions.

● ● ●

from activating to relaxing muscles ("on/off" switches). The more subtle the movements are, the more a rider needs to pay attention to flexibility to avoid "joint lock down" over time from insufficient range of motion in riding. The more the rider's seat is out of the saddle, the more leg-muscle mass is of importance for endurance.

In the Fit to Ride program, these *Discipline Variations* are introduced into the weekly training program in Week 5 after a rider has established a solid base: body balance, flexibility in joints that should be supple, stability around joints that should be stable, spine neutrality, and basic proprioception (body awareness—where you are in space).

Now a rider is ready to train more seriously in other ways because her body is able to handle it without negative compensation or undue wear. All of the training helps a rider find, maintain, and return to a balanced position in which her center of gravity is aligned with the horse's center of gravity (figs. 4.2 A & B).

PART III

Fit to Ride How-To

chapter 5

Nine Weeks to Supple and Straight

The Fit to Ride program is structured to be performed for nine weeks, three times weekly, for approximately 30 minutes duration for each workout. Its main goals are to build the rider a straighter and suppler frame, while improving proprioception, endurance, ability to transfer core strength to movement requirements in the saddle, and creating the simple habit of fitting your exercise into your life.

There is a common training thread throughout the program, which applies to all riders regardless of age, gender, or discipline. However, as mentioned in the last chapter, starting in the Week 5 workout (p. 115), Discipline Variations are offered to help riders further tailor the training to their riding discipline's requirements.

Follow the program through in the order it is presented because each week's exercises establish a foundation for the following week."

While you need to follow the program through in the order it is presented because each week's exercises establish a foundation for the following week, it is not as important to fit the program into nine weeks. For example, if you are very fit and symmetrical, you may find some of the starter exercises quite easy and accomplish that week's entire objective in only one or two days. So, it would be perfectly acceptable to move on to the next week's exercises when you are ready.

Keep in mind that it may be tempting to move too quickly: I often find that when an exercise seems too easy to a client, she is, in fact, not doing it with the correct alignment or technique. Training incorrect technique negatively impacts your preparation for each next stage.

Pace Yourself: It's YOUR Workout

Since this program is all about taking some time out to reset and restart, it is better to go at a measured pace, ensuring correct technique. If most of the exercises in one week's workout are easy except for one or a few, then spend less time on the ones you can master easily, and more time on your problem areas. Sometimes an exercise challenges a rider in an area that is not specifically discussed in the exercise description.

I often get told by clients that their experience of an exercise is different from the description of the muscles that the exercise is mainly working on—especially when they are lacking a base of joint fitness and health in order to do the exercise to its full benefit. This is normal, and happens frequently when a rider has tension, knots, asymmetry, or some difficulty with efficient neuromuscular firing patterns and is retraining muscle memory.

The goal is not to get to the end, get there fast, carry a lot of weight, or log extreme accomplishments. This is not gimmicky fitness-industry training. This is *body conditioning*. The goal is to retrain your body for straightness, symmetry, and movement without blockages. This takes time. It also means working on areas you naturally want to avoid or don't like. If you are over 30 and doing this workout, you have a lifetime of established patterns where your body has found favorite ways to negotiate tasks. To ride better, you need to "untrain" some of these, which means being uncomfortable. It is better to go through this process off the horse, where you can focus on yourself and what you need to do while safely on the ground and can control the factors influencing your body.

Alternatively, some weeks might actually take longer than one week to achieve mastery and comfort with the exercises. When this is the case, take your time before moving forward. For example, if you do an exercise that seems harder for you to do with the left side of your body than the right, keep training it until your weaker side catches up. Doing more on the strong side will worsen the imbalance that has become apparent through the exercise. Rushing can force your body to create compensatory mechanisms or patterns, which are not helpful. *Take your time.*

To help you pace yourself and tailor the program to your own needs, each week of exercises includes *modifications* that you can use to accommodate special considerations such as injury, or need for more advanced work. I call this workout approach the "accordion workout" because it can contract or expand a little within its framework. You can even get more mileage out of it by going through it twice. You can do the basic exercises the first time, and then do the program again, attempting the more advanced suggestions the second time around. Or you can substitute one or two exercises for others you have found elsewhere in your second time through, as long as the substitute exercises work the body in a similar way.

Rhythm is another important aspect of pacing. As with working horses, *working your own body in a steady rhythm* helps muscle memory develop faster, and helps avoid injury. For flexibility exercises, practice combining deep breathing with a regular count to 30, 60, or up to 120 seconds as you flow in and out of the stretch, or hold it for deeper muscle lengthening. For the other exercises, count to 3 or 4 in a steady rhythm as you shift in and out of the exercise. Working

Take your time.
Modify as needed.
Find a steady rhythm."

in a steady rhythm is extremely important for avoiding "cheating" and injury. When you swing in and out of an exercise without rhythm, it is too easy to use compensatory muscles and movement patterns, gravity, or momentum, rather than the muscle pattern the exercise is designed to train. Physically, you cheat yourself out of the full value of the exercise, and you place yourself more at risk of injury. It is better to only do a part of your workout that day if you are squeezed for time, than to rush.

The exercises are grouped so that you can divide the parts of your workout into separate segments and do them at different times if your schedule makes 10 to15 minute slots easier to manage than one single 30- or 40-minute slot.

Reps and Sets

Strength and core-training exercises are divided into *repetitions* ("reps") and *sets*. A *repetition* is performing the movement once. A *set* is a series of repetitions done in one collective block. Some exercises may call for two sets and give a range of repetitions, such as 10 to 12. This means that you do the exercise 10 to 12 times, then rest or do something else (the set is completed) before doing the second set of 10 to 12 repetitions.

Listen to Your Body

While it is normal and desirable to do exercises to a point where they are effective, the exercises should not hurt as you do them. The "no pain, no gain" mantra is old-school, and was surpassed in conditioning best practice long ago. Plus, the fact that you wouldn't apply it to your horse should tell you not to use it on yourself!

While there is a place for ripping muscle fibers and feeling soreness in muscles after some exercises, pain while doing the exercises is usually not a good sign. For example, effective stretches should feel like a "3" to "5" out of "10" on a scale of "feeling it." If you push yourself too much in a stretch, you will create a contracting reaction and can also do damage to the muscle fibers you are gently trying to lengthen. But, if you are too conservative, you will not get the gains that you need in your problem areas.

For strength and endurance exercises, you should be feeling a burn in your muscles and be concentrating and "fighting for it" in your last few repetitions. When it is too easy, you aren't building muscle fiber or endurance. However, you should never feel pain in joints or a muscle tear or twinge while you are training. You need to listen to your *entire* body while you are doing the exercises in order to develop the whole-body-movement awareness needed for riding. If your body tells you some part is bothered significantly by the exercise, listen. Don't brush off that signal. Learning to hear your own body is learning to hear your horse better. If something is not working, check to make sure your technique is correct and be prepared to stop, see a fitness or medical professional or therapist, and discuss the exercise and the problem before proceeding.

When that happens, don't slack off. Do what you can in the meantime to keep your exercise appointment with yourself, and to keep on working on the areas you can work on. "All or nothing'" is also old-school. I have worked with so many people recovering from injury or with disability; they have taught me that you can always choose to do *something* to help your situation, and *something is better than nothing*.

Keys to Success

Three simple tips will help you to achieve success with this program: *plan workout time and space*, *pace yourself*, and *track progress*.

1 | Plan Workout Time and Space

The object of this exercise program is to give you routines you can do within 30 minutes, three times a week. For each of the nine weeks, additional options are also suggested. Remember that at first, your routine will take you more than 30 minutes because you are getting to understand the exercises. Over time, you will become more proficient at setting up your working space and moving through the exercises efficiently. Some riders can schedule more time in a single block. Others find it

easier to break the workout components into sections and do them in 10 to 15 minute blocks at several times during the day.

Whatever you decide to do, make a concrete plan in your agenda for the days and times when you will do your exercises. Be realistic with your time planning. Set a "nice-to-have" goal and a "bare-minimum" goal that will allow you to maintain a sense of progress. Both a vague objective and an over-ambitious plan will sabotage your progress: it is much better to be consistent with a little, and build on that consistency. When planning your workout times, it is normal to find that the first few weeks fluctuate as you develop new physical-training habits and experiment with when they best fit in your schedule. Experimentation is not failure to stick to a plan: it is the road to a plan you can stick to.

It is very helpful to prepare a workout space with the appropriate equipment handy. You would not dream of training your horse in a space in which you could not work him adequately. If you have to constantly look around for your equipment or exercise in a space you detest, change the logistics of your setup. I have discovered, for example, that many clients put exercise equipment in an unfinished basement and then never use it because they just don't want to be in that dark utilitarian place. If all you have is a basement without windows, get a bright lamp. I once converted a garage into a training space by putting a carpet on the floor and hanging posters of Olympic athletes all around the walls. Many clients shift living room furniture temporarily for their exercise. Changing the space by adding light and music can really help.

All of the exercises in this workout plan are designed with minimal space and equipment so that virtually anyone can find a way to complete the program. In some cases, you may find some exercise types are easier to do at home and others at the stable or a nearby park. Schedule accordingly. Being aware of what will work physically for you will help make sticking to your plan easier. Planning your logistics in advance will help eliminate excuses, especially if you are busy.

2 | Pace Yourself

As previously discussed (see p. 52), a steady pace that best suits you may result in taking longer (or slightly less time) to do the program. As long as you are doing the exercise selections that are matched to your ability and master them before moving on, you can adjust the time it takes you to complete your workout. Paying attention to personal weak links is more important when retraining a body for symmetry and a new "physical vocabulary," than speed or strength.

3 | Track Progress

Success with all athletic and personal-fitness programs means writing down what you are doing and making some notes on your progress. By making quick tracking notes, you will be able to see your progress objectively. This is very important, especially at times when you may be less motivated. Some of my training clients have enjoyed using visual formats such as simply writing brief details in a wall calendar, while others use a sheet of paper or software program like Microsoft Excel. Use a system that works for your learning style and that is easy for you to maintain. A very simple system that you use consistently is better than a complicated one that goes by the wayside.

In addition to reminding yourself of how much you are accomplishing, formally writing down your progress will give you valuable information that you can share with your coach, a personal trainer, doctor, or therapist as needed. Key aspects to log are: the exercises you are doing, how many repetitions, how many sets, what weight or resistance you use, and the order you do them in.

Generally, I have organized the exercises in this plan in the order I would advise them to be done in. Different exercise combinations can affect how many of them you can perform, how much weight you can use, or for how long you can do them. If you decide to change the order of exercises within a block, be aware that you may notice changes in how your body responds.

Some riders also find it helpful to keep a journal for the first couple of weeks to note trends that emerge such as the time of day that seems to work best for them. Writing down what you are doing can encourage you when you think your progress is slow. It also allows you to be very individual and pay attention to your personal weak links.

5.1 A & B Your exercise ball should be large enough and firm enough so that you can sit on it with your knees at a 90-degree bend. It is better to have a ball that is slightly large than one that is too small.

• • •

Workout Tools

The Fit to Ride plan is designed to be accessible to a very wide range of riders regardless of discipline, gender, physical ability (or disability), age, level of riding skill, access to a fitness gym, state of mobility (traveling versus fixed location), and socio-economic bracket. The bare essentials are light, inexpensive, and highly portable. Not all of the items on the list are needed for every week's workout.

1 | Comfortable Clothing

Wear clothing that is not too baggy and allows your body to flex and breathe. Exercise-wear of any quality will do, as will riding apparel. Some exercises can be done in regular streetwear, but many require stretch in the fabric so that you are not restricted. Clothing that is baggy can be a nuisance, too hot, and obstruct your ability to monitor your posture and technique.

2 | Exercise Ball

These come in a range of makes, quality, price points, and colors (figs. 5.1 A & B). I have found none of these factors to be relevant to the usefulness of the ball and have used many low-priced balls for years without a

problem. Some of the more expensive ones tend to be too hard or too soft. The right ball should not "squish" excessively when you sit on it but should have some elasticity or give, and not feel hard under your seat. The right size is a ball you can sit on comfortably with a 90-degree bend at the knees. Although this angle is not a hard-and-fast rule and you

5.2 A & B
An inexpensive
mirror can
be placed
in different
positions to help
you monitor your
alignment.

● ● ●

A

B

3 | Portable Mirror

If you do not have mirrors in your training space, it is helpful to purchase one that would go inside a school's full-length clothing locker, or on the back of a bedroom door (figs. 5.2 A & B). These are usually a foot or less in width and about 3 or 4 feet long. They are sold very inexpensively at most outlets that carry household furniture and shelving or back-to-school items.

A light mirror that is not fixed to a wall can be placed at strategic spots in your training area, and moved around easily so that you can monitor your position and technique in various exercises. It can be laid horizontally or propped up vertically as needed, and then stored away easily under a couch, bed, or in a closet when not in use.

4 | Exercise Tubing or Band

Either of these options will work (figs. 5.3 A & B). If you need to purchase an item, I always recommend medium gauge tubing with soft handles. It is available anywhere where basic fitness equipment is sold. Medium-gauge resistance tubing can be used as a single strand or doubled up for harder work. It is very light and portable for riders who travel.

The nylon-webbing handles facilitate various exercises where a loop is placed around your ankle or wrist, or attached to a door knob, railing, post, or piece of furniture. Having tubing with handles is better for some neuromuscular work because unlike the flat therapy band, the rider can hold onto the tube through the handle without actually having to close her hands and grip. But, if you

can work with a ball that is slightly smaller or larger, exercise balls that are too small, too large, too hard, or too soft do not support your lower-back posture correctly during many of the exercises. Since a main goal of this program is to strengthen and ensure health in your back, it is important to have a ball that will help.

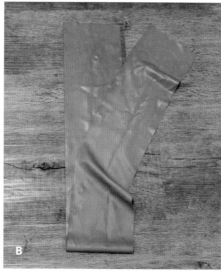

5.3 A & B Ideal exercise tubing is medium strength with soft handles (A). A Theraband™ (B).

● ● ●

already have the flat band material, start out with that and purchase tubing only when you find you cannot make do easily with what you have.

Exercise tubing and exercise balls can last a very long time if you treat them nicely: *do not* subject them to wide temperature fluctuations, and *do* protect them from being scraped or poked by sharp objects, and from getting too hot or too cold. Such conditions degrade the materials and contribute to equipment failure.

5 | Exercise Mat

The best kind of mat for this program is a yoga mat or similar flat mat that offers some cushion but is not so cushioned that your ankles bend significantly while standing on it. It shouldn't be so soft your mother could sleep on it! You need to be able to stand and place your hands on it so that your ankles and wrists are not over-flexed when supporting your weight (figs. 5. 4 A & B). You also need to feel your two seat bones under you when sitting on the mat.

5.4 A & B Your exercise mat should cushion you on the floor (A), but not be too thick (B) because that can cause too much bend in wrists and ankles.

● ● ●

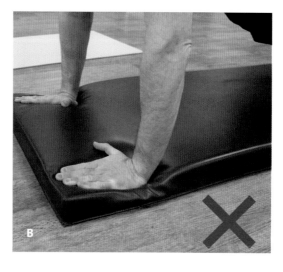

How to Construct a Basic Balance Board

Ideally, construct a basic "balance board" from a piece of wood, plywood, or other material so that it is approximately 24 inches wide (end to end) and deep enough to be longer than your foot (fig. 5.5 A).

1 | Get a plank or piece of plywood that is wide enough for you to stand on it with your feet approximately at the distance they would normally be in the saddle. For exercises, this is normally 2 feet (24 inches). Ideally, the board should also be deep enough so you can stand on it without your feet going over the edge: 1½ feet (18 inches) is a good depth.

2 | Cut a slim piece of wood that is at least the same measurement as the depth of the board—that is, if the board is 18 inches deep, the slim piece should also be 18 inches. The total dimensions of the piece should be approximately 2 inches by 2 inches by 18 inches. It should have flat sides all around.

3 | Draw a vertical and a horizontal line down the exact middle of the main plank so there is a spot right in the middle where the two lines cross. These lines will be where you want your 2 by 2 slim piece to lie.

4 | Line up the 2 by 2 so it is in the dead center of the board—when you stand on it, you will teeter-totter side to side. Attach the 2 by 2 to the board at the center spot (fig. 5.5 B). You can either attach it using just one screw or nail dead center so that it can be "swiveled" along either of the centerlines (permitting balance training side to side *or* front to back), or you can attach the slim piece firmly with multiple nails or screws on the vertical line along the board's depth, as shown in the photos. This allows only training side to side.

An advantage to the firmer attachment is that it is less likely to come apart with use. The lateral, or side-to-side, instability helps riders train the kind of side-to-side symmetry needed for riding. The fact that the slim piece down the middle has a flat bottom is very important because it allows a rider to find a neutral "sweet spot" that she then tries to keep while doing other movements. This mimics the way the rider needs to find and keep neutrality in her core while doing other tasks on the horse.

A

B

6 | Balance Challengers

You can use many different tools for challenging balance. However, it is ideal if you can obtain a simple "balance board." An alternative to buying one is to make it—a great activity for 4-H or Pony Club (see sidebar, p. 60).

Wobble boards, BOSU®, and other balance-training objects are out there on the market, and all balance work helps a rider. However, it's particularly useful to have a balance board that is unstable in only one direction at a time and that has a flat or neutral position. Wobble boards and boards with round forms on the bottom are unbalanced in all directions in a way in which horses are not. They challenge the body to constantly adjust, but do not allow you to obtain a peaceful, still, neutral position.

By using a flat-bottomed, simple balance board, you are challenged to achieve balance and then can work on keeping your weight centered while doing other tasks in a way that is more similar to riding.

Other balance objects that are inexpensive and helpful are: balance cushions, very soft and thick *actual* cushions, a rolled-up towel, a foam pool noodle, and two tennis balls (figs. 5.6 A–G). I very often take two tennis balls with me to clinics to simulate the work that I advise clients to do on a balance board, because tennis balls are so small and easy to pack and store.

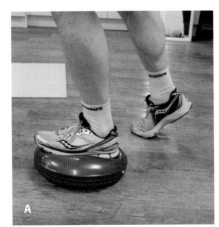

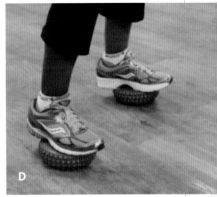

5.6 A–G Balance cushions (A & B); balance pods (C & D); tennis balls (E & F); pool noodle (G).

●●●

Safety Considerations

To a certain extent, all exercise has inherent risk. In addition to their suitability for the Fit to Ride workout, the exercises in this plan have also been selected for their general safety and the ease with which they can be undertaken on your own. As each individual's needs and limitations are different, it is important here to restate the previous caution that none of the exercises should be painful. If they are, or if you feel joint or other strain or pains that seem unusual, stop the exercise and consult your doctor, physical therapist, or coach. Normal attention to technique and posture

with healthy joint function should result in pain-free exercise. Other safety tips for a great workout are:

1 | Drink water before you train and any time you need it through the workout. Dehydration causes neuromuscular response delays, which will impact your timing: Your brain-to-muscle connection gets broken or delayed since it is effectively an electrical impulse signal that requires hydration for conductivity. Staying hydrated is especially important in hot weather or in dry climates (either hot or cold).

2 | Eat something or drink juice in the half-hour before you do any moderate-to-intense training, including riding. Training with low blood sugar causes your core and stabilizing muscles to be weak and less supportive of your spine and other joints. Your response times are also negatively affected by low blood sugar. The horse notices a response-time lag long before you do.

3 | Declutter your training area. Just like your barn aisle, it's important to make sure there aren't any items you can step on, get caught up in, have fall on you, roll underfoot, or any similar misadventures. Keep the equipment you need handy, but remember to move weights or balls to the side where they aren't in your way when you are not using them.

4 | Monitor rubber/latex equipment such as exercise balls, balance cushions, and exercise tubing for tears or wear, and try to protect

---

10 Tips for a Safe Workout

1 | Drink water.

2 | Eat something light in the hour beforehand.

3 | Declutter the workout area.

4 | Monitor equipment for damage.

5 | Familiarize yourself with the equipment prior to using it.

6 | Take your time.

7 | Train in a steady rhythm.

8 | Manage injury or medical conditions by doing *less* than you think you can get away with.

9 | Monitor for correct position.

10 | Do not attempt exercises on your horse that are intended to be done on the ground.

them from wild swings in temperature. Do not use them when they are freezing cold. Tears, temperature swings, and extreme temperatures can compromise the integrity of the material thus creating risk of it breaking or bursting while you are using it. Under normal conditions, these items can withstand many workouts a week, for several years.

5 | If you are unfamiliar with the fitness ball or other balance-challenging tools, ease your way into learning how to balance on them before performing the indicated exercises. Also, it is not a crime—and is not cheating—to hold the back of a chair, a railing, or balance yourself with a hand on a wall or the floor if you need to, in order to "mount" and "dismount" from these items safely, and perform the exercise.

6 | Take your time. If some of the exercises are targeting muscles and muscle combinations that are not used to working in the way you are asking them, your body-response times will be slower. Taking your time ensures you can connect with the right areas and train them to respond. Rushing results in compensatory patterns or puts you at risk for lack of joint or spine support.

7 | Move with a relaxed and steady rhythm. Rushing, swinging, or lurching into and out of an exercise can put you at risk for straining something.

8 | When you have an injury or other condition, err on the side of a "too light" workout, and slowly ramp yourself up to give time for the injured or imbalanced areas to gradually catch up. Overdoing it will not get you there faster. As many marathon runners and endurance riders I know like to say, "Go slow to go fast."

9 | Monitor yourself in a mirror to ensure good posture, or get a friend or coach to help you double-check your posture and technique. Monitoring your technique is especially important if you are finding that an exercise seems to "work" an area you didn't expect, seems too easy, or when you have an injury or other condition.

10 | Resist the temptation to try ground-based exercises on your horse. The reason they are ground-based is so you can move your limbs in a range of motion and use resistance loads not always possible to do on the horse, as well as concentrate on what you are doing. If you are inspired to try different stretches and coordination maneuvers on your horse, please be sure you have taken all the normal safety precautions for vaulting or longe work under instruction or with appropriately trained side handlers/monitors. Unfamiliar movements and exercise equipment can spook even the quietest horse.

PART IV

The 9-Week Fit to Ride Program

Before You Begin

All the Fit to Ride daily workouts are presented so that they can be completed in one time block or in separate time blocks, depending on your scheduling needs. Within each week's three-day program, Day One of the new routine is about *learning* the new exercises for that week. On Day Two, you *perfect* your technique. On Day Three, you can *add* repetitions or *change* weight loads.

Generally, give yourself at least a one-day break in between each of the three weekly workout days (if you are doing all the exercise blocks in the same day) unless otherwise indicated. If you split the blocks, ensure that you have a day between—for example, if you do most of your exercises in one day, but your strength training or cardiovascular workout section the next day, keep this pattern so that no two same blocks are repeated on back-to-back days (again, unless otherwise indicated). Stretches can be done every day, and multiple times a day. Core training can be done daily, as well.

Depending on your particular training needs as regards symmetry and stamina, you may find that this process takes longer in some weeks than others. This is why I recommend that you remain in a specific "week" of the program until you have achieved mastery of the exercises and are ready for the next week's workout. Of course, taking the extra time you need can result in the program taking you longer than nine weeks overall.

Each daily workout is organized into several parts:

1 | Warm-Up
2 | Core Training Exercises
3 | Strength & Muscle Memory Exercises
4 | Deep Stretching
5 | Stamina & Coordination

Also included at the end of many of the exercises are adaptations: *Special Needs Modifications* (for riders with specific difficulties or less athletic ability) and *Advanced Exercise Variations* (for riders who feel they can go further with the exercise).

Summary of the Three Weekly Workouts

Day 1: Learn new exercises.

Day 2: Perfect the routine.

Day 3: Add difficulty through more weight or more reps.

chapter 6

Standard
Warm-Up Stretches

This warm-up routine should be completed before each workout (and also before riding). As you get familiar with these exercises, you will find this routine goes very quickly. I recommend you repeat each exercise 3 to 6 times, depending on how stiff you are feeling that day.

Most exercises start with you in a *spine-neutral rider position* (legs apart, knees bent, spine and pelvis straight, core engaged), unless otherwise indicated. None of the exercises are done with the knees locked because a straight, locked leg tilts the pelvis forward, breaks spine neutrality, and disengages important posture-supporting core muscles.

6.1 A Shoulder Rotations.

● ● ●

Shoulder Rotations

Purpose: To loosen the shoulders and chest area (*pectorals*—see fig. 3.19 D, p. 44).

Shoulder rotations come in many forms. Rolling shoulders back and swinging an arm or both arms around in full backward circles are two of them. This particular version is designed to help stretch the *minor pectoral*

and the shoulder rotator cuff muscles, which commonly cause a rider's chest to collapse.

1 | Hold a lead shank, long whip, or similar object in front of you, arms set wide apart (fig. 6.1 A).

2 | Raise it up overhead, taking a deep breath to relax your back and shoulder muscles (figs. 6.1 B & C).

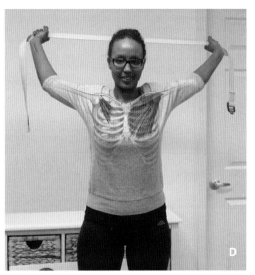

3 | Continue the motion bringing the lead or whip down behind you (figs. 6.1 D & E).

4 | Take a deep breath while returning the whip or lead up over your head and to its original position in front of you. Repeat several times in rhythm.

If your shoulders are very tight, you may not be able to complete the motion fully. In this case, you may need to have a very wide grip, or adjust your position to bring the lead or whip overhead and behind you, one arm at a time. Maintain a two-handed grip, even if you need to wiggle, bend your elbows, or otherwise maneuver.

Side Bends

Purpose: To stretch the *obliques* and *latissimus dorsi* (figs. 3.13 A–C and 3.21 B, pp. 29 and 46).

Side Bends release your *obliques, latissimus dorsi,* and *intercostal* (between the ribs, under the obliques) muscles to allow freedom of movement in your shoulders and hips.

1 | Stand with your legs at approximately a shoulder-width with knees slightly bent so that your spine and pelvis are in neutral upright posture.

2 | Engage your *abdominals* slightly to support a neutral spine through the movement.

3 | Flow back and forth over each side, reaching your arm over your head to loosen your hips, maintaining alignment—no tipping forward or back—and keeping your pinky up and thumb down to align your arm (fig. 6.2).

Imagine you are curving around a ball to keep aligned and stretch through your ribs. Reach into the stretch while almost pushing your ribs in the opposite direction until you feel the stretch along your ribs, as well.

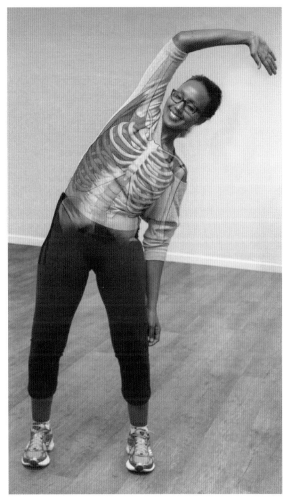

6.2 Side Bends.

● ● ●

Engage the Abdominals

You can engage your abdominals by imagining that you are pulling your bellybutton up slightly. You can check to see if your abdominals are engaged by placing your hands on your waist. Your waist should feel like it presses out at you slightly. It is incorrect to try and engage abdominal muscles by sucking in your belly.

Neck Stretch

Purpose: To stretch neck muscles, including the *trapezius* (see fig. 3.18 A, p. 42).

Believe it or not, stretching your neck muscles makes a difference, even though we do not see riders craning their necks very often! Stretching your neck actually stretches the *levator scapula* as well as the *trapezius* muscles (see figure referenced above), in addition to neck muscles. If you carry tension in your shoulders and neck, this exercise is especially important, but if you are relaxed and supple, doing quick neck stretches will just be part of healthy spine maintenance.

● ● ●
6.3 Neck Stretch.

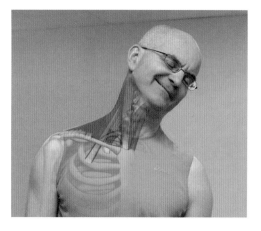

1 | Holding your arms down to keep your shoulders down, tilt your head from side to side, bringing your ear toward your shoulder with a deep breath each time (fig. 6.3).

2 | You can also tuck your head forward as if looking under your armpit on each side.

Do not roll your head back because this compresses your neck vertebrae. If you have a lot of tension in your neck and shoulders, you can help release it by taking a free hand and squeezing your *trapezius* muscle or pushing down on it gently as you lean into the stretch. Do not hold the stretch very long before switching to the other side. These stretches should be done fairly slowly and rhythmically.

A rider with shoulder tension can do this stretch, holding it longer, at the end of the day. When doing a deep neck stretch (any stretch can be turned into a "deep" one by holding it longer), it is important to use your hand to help raise your head afterward, since a deep stretch in the neck muscles will stretch the fibers and you can strain something by trying to lift the weight of your head using the same muscles that you just elongated.

Fold and Roll

Purpose: To stretch the lower back area and *hamstrings* (see sidebar, pp. 36–7) while mobilizing the spine.

This stretch sequence combines a *hamstring stretch*, with a spine flexion to mobilize it. It could also be called Toe Touch with Roll Up.

1 | Start with legs at shoulder-width and spine neutral as previously discussed: knees bent slightly and core engaged without hollowing or slouching the back.

●●●
6.4 A–F
Fold and Roll.

2 | Straighten your back and fold forward as far as you can with your back straight, until you feel a pull or stretch happening up the back of your legs. One useful way to achieve this without cheating by rounding your back is to imagine you are diving forward with your chest (like a swan dive). Depending on where you are tight, the stretch might localize at any point from your heel to your seat, or might include the whole muscle chain (fig. 6.4 A).

3 | Do not compromise your spine neutrality (flatness of your back in this case). The goal is not to touch your toes, but to properly fold at the pelvis to achieve a complete stretch of the *hamstrings*. You can place your hands on your thighs to help keep your back flat.

4 | Stay in the stretch moment for only one count, then bend your knees, flop your back down, then slowly roll upward into the upright position again. Breathe deeply to relax your spine and rib muscles (figs. 6.4 B–F).

Special Needs Modification
Standing Hamstring Stretch

This modification is useful as a warmup or a stretch modification when you are so tight in the hamstrings that the Fold and Roll exercise does not work well for you. Use this modification when you cannot get very far when you try to touch your toes or your back is rounded when you do so, or if you become dizzy with toe-touch type exercises and raising your head up and down.

1 | Stand with good posture in front of an object that's roughly at knee height.

2 | Prop one foot up on the object, with a straight leg. Place your hands on your upper thigh.

6.5 Standing Hamstring Stretch.

● ● ●

Flat Back

I use the term "flat back" rather than "straight back" more often because many people associate straightness with vertical posture. If you look at fig. 6.5, the back is in a line from the rider's shoulder to pelvis: it is flat—as opposed to rounded or hollow. It is technically straight, but since many people would look at the picture and not see an upright back, they get confused.

Note that the bend should be happening at the hip joint, not through a series of vertebrae. The spine, of course, is not perfectly flat since an apparently flat back only appears so because of musculature. The spine is naturally slightly curved in an "S," even when perfectly balanced and neutral.

3 | Using your arms to help you maintain position, make sure your back is absolutely straight and lean forward. You should have a feeling of sticking your chest and backside out a little. Reach your chest toward your foot and your stomach toward your knee. It may help you to reach for your toe with one hand, once you have properly organized your back to remain flat and straight (fig. 6.5).

4 | Stop reaching at the point at which you feel a stretch up the back of your extended leg.

When using this modification prior to exercising (or riding), only hold the position for a second before releasing, relaxing, and repeating. For a deep stretch at the end of your day, hold the position for several deep breaths before relaxing and repeating.

Round and Hollow

Purpose: To mobilize the spine while opening up the chest and *hip flexors* (*psoas*—see figs. 2.3 A & B, p. 20).

This stretch is for the small muscles around your spine (*multifidi*) and to achieve healthy movement in your spine (see fig. 3.1 B, p. 27). It is a great exercise to do immediately after Fold and Roll to continue the spine mobility that you began there.

1 | Bring your arms forward and roll your upper back into a ball by flexing, slouching, or rounding it (fig. 6.6 A).

2 | Lift yourself up and open your chest as you curve yourself backward, extending your spine. Open your hands outward (thumbs back) and bring your chin up (fig. 6.6 B).

Take care to keep your hips slightly back and engage your *abdominals* so that you protect your lower back. Riders who need this exercise the most tend to have a stiff upper back and compensate by bending too much in the lower back. You should not feel any pain—or a lot of bend—in your lower back, since the goal is to isolate your upper back (the thoracic region of the spine).

6.6 A & B Round and Hollow.

● ● ●

Hip Flexor to Ankle Stretch (Lunge and Press)

Purpose: To stretch *psoas, quadriceps,* calf muscles, and Achilles tendon (see sidebar, p. 36–7, and figs. 3.15 A & B, p. 38).

1 | Lunge forward to stretch your hip flexors *(psoas),* keeping your head and torso upright and hips, knees, toes, and shoulders facing forward. You can hold a solid object for balance. You should feel the stretch in the upper thigh at the crease with your hip in the hip flexor area (fig. 6.7 A).

2 | As you come out of the forward phase of the stretch, press your heel back onto the ground to stretch your Achilles tendon (ankle area). Make sure that your feet are pointed forward so that the alignment forces your calf and Achilles tendon to stretch (fig. 6.7 B).

Those who need this stretch combination the most find that they cannot go very deeply into it. Do not compromise your lower back. Do not overdo the lunge phase of the stretch, and do not worry if you cannot touch your heel to the ground in the press-back phase.

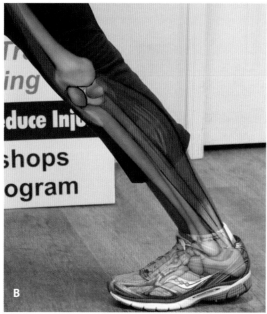

6.7 A & B Hip Flexor to Ankle Stretch.

• • •

Gentle Repetition, *Not* Force

Diligent, gentle, repeated, and regular use of these stretches will gradually improve your flexibility. Forcing stretches does *not* help: it just tears, rather than lengthening, muscle fiber.

Ankle Circles

Purpose: To mobilize ankles for better absorption of the horse's movement and better leg position.

1 | Stand on one leg (with a slightly bent knee) and lift your other foot off the ground (fig. 6.8 A).

2 | Roll your foot in slow circles in one direction (fig. 6.8 B).

3 | Repeat in the other direction, and with the other foot.

6.8 A & B Ankle Circles.

● ● ●

Side-to-Side Lunge

Purpose: To stretch *adductors* (inner thighs—see fig. 2.4, p. 20).

This stretch is particularly helpful for riders with chair-seat tendencies, as well as those who have difficulty sitting more deeply in the saddle. However, all riders can benefit. Loosening the inner-thigh area helps release the hips to follow the horse's motion, as well as permitting a more neutral leg position.

1 | Start with legs quite wide, aiming your seat bones back and down to open up your hips, and stretch the inner thighs.

2 | Shift your weight to one side (one leg bent, one leg straight, hips more over one foot than the other), until you feel a stretch in the inner-thigh and groin area (fig. 6.9).

6.9 Side-to-Side Lunge.

● ● ●

6.10 Side-to-Side Lunge Holding an Object.

● ● ●

3 | Shift back and forth with a deep breath each time. Flow back and forth in a continuous, slow motion rather than holding the stretch on one side or the other. (As soon as you can feel it on one side, start flowing to the other side.) Only stretch your legs as wide as you need to— to feel the stretch.

Special Needs Modification
Side-to-Side Lunge Holding an Object

Holding onto something for balance as you perform your inner-thigh stretches is not cheating. In fact, if you are very tight in these areas, supporting yourself on an exercise ball, chair, or wall can help you distribute the bodyweight-bearing task to your arms, which will help your hips and thighs relax more.

Week One

Theme: Establishing a stretch routine and incorporating core training.

Equipment Needed: Exercise tubing or lead rope, mat, exercise ball.

Introduction: This week, your Standard Warm-Up Stretches should have become familiar and you can now use them to prepare your body to do core training, which, this week, focuses on foundational postures and movement, as well as getting in the habit of a regular workout. As a bonus, you also start to tackle deeper stretches for areas that are commonly tight for riders, such as the hamstrings.

WEEK ONE AT-A-GLANCE	
Warm-Up	Standard Warm-Up Stretches: Shoulder Rotations, Side Bends, Neck Stretch, Fold and Roll, Round and Hollow, Hip Flexor to Ankle Stretches, Ankle Circles, Side-to-Side Lunge.
Core Training	Floor Crunches, Crossover Crunches, Isometric Crunch with Alternate Arm Shift-Backs.
Strength & Muscle Memory	None.
Deep Stretching	Lying Hamstring Stretch.
Stamina & Coordination	10 minutes walking, 3 times per week.
Special Needs Modifications	Hold an object for the lunge stretches; do a Standing Hamstring Stretch instead of Lying.
Advanced Variations	20–30 reps of the Core Exercises or 2 sets Ball Crunches.
Notes	Establish Standard Stretch routine, then do Lying Hamstring Stretch. Day 1: Stretch and walk only. Day 2: Stretches will go faster and you can add the Core Training exercises.

WARM-UP

Perform the Standard Warm-Up Stretches (see p. 67).

CORE TRAINING

Floor Crunches

Goal: 20–30 reps or one set of as many as you can to fatigue.

Muscles Worked: Rectus abdominis.

This basic crunch exercise is the foundation of other core-training exercises. Learning to position your spine and engage your core so that your spine and pelvis are neutral creates muscle memory and an engagement pattern that you can transfer to all other floor and standing core exercises, as well as movement with *integrated core* engagement (see sidebar, p. 79).

When this exercise is easy for you and you are quite certain you have the correct technique, you can replace it with the Advanced Variation.

1 | Lie on the mat with your knees bent, then tuck in your pelvis slightly to reduce the hollow in your lower back by engaging your abdominals. You should not be able to slide a hand between your lower back and the floor.

2 | Support your neck and head with your hands, and lift your head and shoulder blades off the ground by using your abdominals to shorten the space between your bottom rib and hip bone (fig. 7.1).

3 | Hold for 1 to 3 seconds, and slowly lower yourself to floor, one vertebra at a time.

Speed is not your goal. Performing the exercise slowly will cause your abdominals to be under load for a prolonged period, building endurance. Speed just uses momentum and robs you of the benefits for building abdominal endurance.

Advanced Variation
Try the Ball Crunches from Week 2 (see p. 87).

Crossover Crunches

Goal: 20 reps (left and right equals one rep).

Muscles Worked: Rectus abdominis, obliques.

Once you have mastered the basic position, this exercise adds an element of asymmetrical loading and cross-body movement.

1 | Position yourself as for a basic Floor Crunch (see p. 78) and raise your body off the floor in the same matter. Ensure that you are straight and symmetrical.

2 | Reach one hand and arm toward your knee and tap or touch the outside of your knee, then cross over and reach the other hand and arm to the opposite knee (figs. 7.2 A & B).

3 | Return to your start position between each rep. Make sure that you feel a squeeze in your *obliques* (near the ribs on one side) and that you otherwise maintain symmetry and alignment. Crossing your body with a good effort is more important than actually reaching your knees. Again, compromising alignment with speed will reduce the effectiveness of the exercise. You should not be wiggling, and your hips and legs should not be moving.

7.2 A & B Crossover Crunches.

● ● ●

Integrated Core

What does this mean? It indicates your core is engaged while you are doing other exercises (as opposed to your core itself being the main target of an exercise). The goal for riders is to be able to transfer targeted core work to integrated core usage because that is how your body organizes itself while you are riding.

The ideal is to train your core well enough that you rarely ever have to think about it while riding because your body automatically engages it correctly, and you have built up the strength and stamina that permits you to focus on riding, not on which muscles in your body are properly engaged.

Isometric Crunch with Alternate Arm Shift-Backs

Goal: 10–15 reps (left and right equals one rep).

Muscles Worked: Transverse abdominis, lower back muscles, latissimus dorsi.

This exercise finishes off working your *abdominals* by adding extra endurance and asymmetrical loading when they have already been fatigued from the previous exercises.

1 | Get into a basic crunch position then perform the crunch, holding your head and shoulders off the ground (fig. 7. 3 A).

2 | Free one arm and reach it overhead behind you, holding the raised position with your arm extended for 1 to 3 seconds. Hold your opposite arm where it feels most comfortable (fig. 7.3 B).

3 | Return your hands to their starting position behind your head and neck, and repeat on the other side.

4 | Slowly roll yourself back onto the floor, breathe, engage your abdominals and repeat.

When your lower back begins to lift off the floor, release from the exercise and rest. As you get more advanced, you can add difficulty by holding a weight in your reaching hand.

● ● ●

7.3 A & B
Isometric Crunch with Arm Shift-Backs.

DEEP STRETCHES

Lying Hamstring Stretch

Purpose: Stretches the *hamstrings*, calf, and Achilles tendon, and even the lower-back area.

1 | Lie on your back with knees bent to neutralize the position of your lower back (no excessive hollowing of the lower back).

2 | Lift one leg and loop a lead rope, yoga strap, or exercise tube over your foot so that you can hold your leg in place with your arms while perfectly relaxing your leg.

3 | Straighten the leg that you are holding with the strap. Using your arms, lift the leg into the air until you feel a stretch up the back of the leg. Your free leg can be bent or extended, depending on what's most comfortable (fig. 7.4).

4 | When you can feel a level of stretch that is about a "3" or "4" out of "10," hold this position. Breathe deeply until the feeling of stretch diminishes.

5 | Use the strap to raise your leg slightly higher until you can feel more of a stretch.

Your knee can be straight, or slightly bent, whichever is more comfortable. Do not overdo it. If you are particularly tight in the hamstrings, you will need to stay in this exercise for 2 to 5 minutes to get the full

benefit. Go very slowly, increasing the stretch by small increments. Aggressively pulling your leg up until you feel pain will not help your muscles and ligaments get more supple. It will tear them. Aggressive or too-quick stretching also triggers contraction in the muscle you are trying to stretch.

7.4 Lying Hamstring Stretch.

● ● ●

Special Modification
Do the Standing Hamstring Stretch (p. 72).

Slow, Patient Stretching

When stretching, "Pain equals no gain." Be kind and patient with your body. People who need the stretching the most often have the least patience for it. Making yourself slow down to do what you need to do is good mental training. When you start to feel the benefits of being more supple and less tense, you will be converted to regular stretching.

Week Two

Theme: Building on the base of core engagement and flexibility, and testing symmetry.

Equipment Needed: Exercise ball, mat, lead rope or tubing, hand weights.

Introduction: This week, you take your spine off the floor and introduce an opportunity to maintain spine neutrality when gravity is working against you. You'll focus on how to use a ball to get a deeper hip-flexor stretch.

Note for Special Modification Riders
For those who have discovered especially tight areas, you should continue to use the Standard Warm-Up Stretches (p. 67), and dedicate this week to regular intensive stretching of one of the particular areas.

Note for Advanced Variation Riders
Perform this week's exercises in a continuous loop and at a steady but faster rhythm so that your heart rate is elevated, without compromising your technique. See how many sets you can fit into 20 minutes.

WEEK TWO AT-A-GLANCE	
Warm-Up	Standard Stretch routine and one set from the Core Training routine from Week One.
Core Training	Bird Dog variations on all fours, with individual limb reaches, then opposite limb reaches. Starfish—Isometric Crunch with Limb Reaches. Ball Crunches.
Strength & Muscle Memory	Seat Walking on Floor for hip mobility, Standing Deadlifts, Backstep Lunge with Overhead Reach.
Deep Stretching	Spend some extra time in one stretch each day, for your tightest area.
Stamina & Coordination	5 minutes cardiovascular intervals prior to each workout.
Special Needs Modifications	If you are still wobbly on the fitness ball, practice a few crunches on it to gradually gain your balance, and complete your crunch routine on the floor on a balance cushion.
Advanced Variations	Ball Crunches with Isometric Reaches.
Notes	Focus this week on stretching one area intensively, and learning how to use objects such as a bench or ball to get deeper hip-flexor stretch.

WARM-UP

This week introduces use of some light cardio-vascular exercise to warm up your muscles.

1 | Prior to starting the new exercises for this week, complete the Standard Warm-Up Stretches (p. 67) and do one set of one of the Core Training exercises you learned in Week One (p. 77).

2 | Now finish your warm-up by straightening and stretching your core, lying on the ground with your arms overhead, resting on the ground. Rest your arms on a cushion or stool if they cannot comfortably relax on the ground. Take two to three breaths, stretching your body as long as you can from the tip of your fingers to your feet, with a moment of relaxation in between.

3 | Do 5 minutes of cardio training. You can jog and walk, walk with intervals of added vigorous arm movement, bicycle, use cardio equipment, walk up and down stairs, or walk on the spot alternating with high leg elevations or arm movements to create intensity intervals. After you are thoroughly warmed up, you can proceed to the exercises for this week.

CORE TRAINING

Bird Dog—Single Limb (All Fours)

Goal: 6–10 reps.

Muscles Worked: Transverse abdominis, gluteus maximus, shoulder rotators, latissimus dorsi, deltoids.

The Bird Dog variations are intended to introduce asymmetrical loading to your back. These exercises also train muscle memory and muscle-firing patterns for the chain of muscles that stabilize your torso laterally and that help you control the placement of your shoulders and hips.

The goal of all the variations is to keep your spine neutral, using the floor under you to make sure your shoulders and hips are straight or square to the floor, even when you raise a limb. Training your body off the floor, but still using the floor to help you achieve straightness, prepares you for later freestanding work by training proprioception for true alignment.

1 | Start by positioning yourself on all fours so that you feel even pressure between both knees and both hands. Achieve a neutral spine by hollowing and raising your back repeatedly with gradually smaller movement until you can feel that mid-point where you are neither rounding your back, nor allowing it to sag.

2 | Once you are in a spine-neutral position, raise an arm and hold it for three seconds before resting and repeating (the same arm) 6 to 10 times (fig. 8.1 A).

3 | Do this exercise with the other arm (fig. 8.1 B).

4 | Repeat with each leg. With the legs, pay special attention to not allowing your lower back to hollow. The goal is not to raise your leg high in the air, but to use your *gluteals, hamstrings,* and *back* while maintaining a neutral spine (figs. 8.1 C & D).

Done correctly, you should feel the need to increase your *abdominal use* the higher you lift an arm or leg in order to maintain spine neutrality. The "top" of the movement is the point at which you still have a neutral spine, but you feel as if your body is having an internal tug of war between your core and the muscles used to raise the limb.

● ● ●

8.1 A–D Bird Dog—Single Limb

Bird Dog—Opposite Pair

Goal: 10–15 reps.

Muscles Worked: Same as Bird Dog—Single Limb (p. 83).

Once you have mastered your spine stability and core engagement during the Bird Dog variations raising a single limb, you are ready to add coordination, balance, and the complexity of cross-body training by raising opposite limb pairs (fig. 8.2). Again, perform all the repetitions for one pair before switching to the other pair.

8.2 Bird Dog—Opposite Pair.

● ● ●

Special Needs Modification
Bird Dog with Bent Elbow or on Stool/Ball

If you have a shoulder impingement or lower back pain, you will need to be more conservative with this exercise. You can achieve the physical value of the exercise without lifting your arm as high, by bending your elbow or knee and raising it as far as you can without losing the straightness of your lower back (fig. 8.3 A). If your lower back falls down, you have gone too far with the lift.

Riders with wrist problems can also do the exercise on a stool or ball (fig. 8.3 B). When using a ball, rather than a more stable stool, lift only one limb at a time to maintain your balance.

8.3 A & B Bird Dog with Bent Elbow or on Stool/Ball.

● ● ●

Advanced Variation
Bird Dog with Weight

Once you are comfortable raising the weight of your arm, you can add a weight.

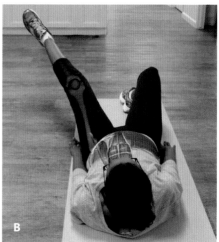

Starfish—Isometric Crunch with Limb Reach

Goal: 6 reps per limb.

Muscles Worked: *Rectus abdominis, transverse abdominis, obliques, hip flexors (psoas), lower abdominal and back muscle area.*

Similarly to the Bird Dog exercises (pp. 83–5), this exercise also trains cross-body strength and stability, but now with your backside on the floor.

1 | Lie on the ground in the position for starting a basic crunch.

● ● ●
8.4 A–C
Starfish—
Isometric
Crunch
with Limb
Reach.

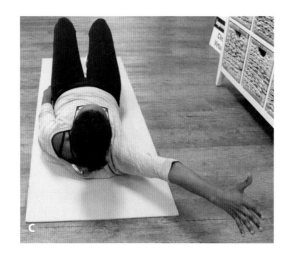

2 | Perform the crunch and hold the position at the top of the movement (head and shoulders off the ground—see p. 78).

3 | While holding the position with your *abs*, extend a limb out on a slight angle from your body (think of a starfish's arms) and continue to hold for 3 to 5 seconds (figs. 8.4 A & B).

4 | Return to neutral (lying on the floor) and repeat with another limb (fig. 8.4 C).

Work your way around until you have used all four limbs. The exercise should be done quite slowly with an emphasis on maintaining core engagement with a neutral spine as you switch from supporting one limb to the next. Your body will be tempted to tilt to one side or another as you switch limbs. Preventing tilting or leaning is where the exercise works. Be as straight, stable, and symmetrical as you can. It may not feel like a dramatic exercise, but the asymmetrical loading will be giving your deep spine stabilizers a pretty hefty workout.

Ball Crunches

Goal: 20–30 reps.

Muscles Worked: Rectus abdominis, transverse abdominis, obliques.

The goal of using the ball is to allow your head and shoulders to drop below the level of your stomach, so that your body has to work harder to lift them up.

1 | Start by sitting on the ball, then roll down until you are lying on it with the ball in the small of your back.

2 | Perform a crunch as you do on the floor (p. 78). At the top of the movement, you should be fairly level as shown in the picture and you should feel that your abs are definitely working (fig. 8.5).

You will also have to focus on lifting up your hips. The *rectus abdominis* connects from the bottom of your rib area to the pubic bone. If you let your seat sit, you will disengage the lower part of the muscle and the exercise will feel easy. If you have uneven strength in your *abdominals*, it will show up in this exercise because the ball will roll a little. Do the crunches with as little wobble as possible. If you have asymmetrical abdominal strength, this is an excellent exercise for retraining symmetry.

8.5 Ball Crunches.

● ● ●

Special Needs Modification
Ball Crunches on Balance Cushion

If you do not yet have your balance on the ball for a crunch, you can still introduce a balance element by doing the crunch on a balance cushion, flat pillow, flake of hay, or other lower-profile item for challenging your balance. The goal is to achieve symmetry, and use the raised surface to be able to stretch your torso longer before performing the lift in the crunch (fig. 8.6).

8.6 Ball Crunches on Balance Cushion.

● ● ●

8.7 Ball Crunches with Isometric Reach.

● ● ●

Advanced Variation
Ball Crunches with Isometric Reaches

For added difficulty, this exercise combines the Ball Crunch with the Starfish from this week.

1 │ Perform a regular Ball Crunch (p. 87) but hold your contracted position.

2 │ Once your shoulders are lifted and your *abdominals* engaged, reach an arm out to the side or back behind you (fig. 8.7). Hold your opposite arm where it feels most comfortable and helps you balance on the ball. Aim for a count of 3 to 5 before releasing the crunch and repeating.

The goal of the exercise is to introduce instability to this already asymmetrical task. If you have asymmetrical core strength, or a tendency for one side to dominate, it should show up in this exercise: you may find one side easier to do than another or that the ball rolls or shakes slightly. Practice over time until you can do the exercise without any change to the position of your torso or the ball.

STRENGTH & MUSCLE MEMORY

Seat Walking on Floor

Goal: 6–10 steps forward and backward.

Muscles Worked: Lower abdominals, obliques, erector spinae muscles controlling hip movement while maintaining upper body posture.

This is a fun little exercise to encourage hip mobility and train your body to shift a hip while keeping a stable upper body position.

1 | Sit on the floor with your legs out in front of you and your back as straight as possible. You may use your hands on the floor to push your torso into a nice upright position. Feel the core muscles you need to engage to keep this position.

2 | Once you are straight, lift one seat bone off the floor and "walk" it forward an inch or two. Make smaller movements if you are stiff (fig. 8.8 A).

3 | Lower your weight onto this seat bone and lift the other one. In this way, you walk along the floor using mostly your *obliques* and other core muscles to lift and shift your hips (fig. 8.8 B).

If you have very tight *hamstrings*, this exercise may be difficult, so start out by sitting at the join of the floor and a wall to train your body into an upright position and teach your body to move away from the wall without losing your upright position.

8.8 A & B Seat Walking on Floor.

● ● ●

Deadlifts—Standing

Goal: 10–12 reps.

Muscles Worked: Gluteus maximus, hamstrings, erector spinae, transverse abdominis, quadriceps.

Deadlifts strengthen your entire "backline" of muscles, which correspond to the muscles you train in your horse. In a sedentary society, this exercise is especially helpful to riders because they frequently have insufficient base strength for supporting their lower spine. This base strength comes from the *gluteals* and lower back.

1 │ Stand with your legs at shoulder-width apart, knees slightly bent and spine neutral, arms dangling down. If you add weight, use the weight load that you can manage without compromising back straightness or having to "muscle" the weights with your arms (fig. 8.9 A).

2 │ Tip forward, allowing the weights to shift as you grasp them at the end of relaxed arms. Ideally, you will tip forward until your back is level with the floor, and your arms are dangling directly down from your chest area (figs. 8.9 B & C).

3 │ Bend your knees slightly and shift your weight back into your *gluteals* (your behind and heels), and lift your torso back up to the starting position. The challenge is to keep your back straight the whole time, and not allow any folding, collapsing, or rounding of the spine (figs. 8.9 D & E).

● ● ●

8.9 A–E Deadlifts—Standing.

You will find that the lower you tip, the more you need to bend your knees and stick your seat back, and the more your back will be engaged. As you tip, you use gravity to bring the workout farther up your back toward your neck. If you have weak back muscles—that is, your back starts to round and you just cannot straighten it—you have tipped too far for your strength level.

Back Step Lunge with Overhead Reach

Goal: 5–10 reps each side.

Muscles Worked: Gluteus maximus, hamstrings, quadriceps, erector spinae, deltoids, latissimus dorsi, transverse abdominis.

The first goal of this exercise is to continue to train correct folding at the hip, while building *quadriceps* (thigh) and *gluteal* strength. The other goals are: to increase your ability to engage your back muscles in integrated movement; improve shoulder strength; and increase your body's vocabulary for multitasking. Yes, these are a lot of accomplishments for one simple exercise!

1 | Start by standing in your athletic-neutral stance: legs wide, knees slightly bent, core engaged, spine neutral.

2 | Shift your weight almost completely onto one foot as you hinge at the hips slightly forward (fig. 8.10 A).

3 | Now that you have freed one foot from weight-bearing, reach it back until you can touch the floor with your toe behind you and descend into a lunging position (figs. 8.10 B & C).

4 | Ensure that most of your weight is on the front thigh—the one you shifted your weight to in the first place.

8.10 A–D Back Step Lunge with Overhead Reach.

5 | Once you are in the lunge position, reach your arms up directly overhead to stretch your torso upright using your back and shoulder muscles. If you have impinged shoulders, you will not be able to lift your arms high. This is okay: the movement and coordination are the important parts of this exercise. If you are quite athletic, you may wish to hold free weights to add to the workload for your shoulders (fig. 8.10 D).

Only use an amount of arm lift (or weights) that allows you to maintain good form in the exercise. You should not be wobbling or weaving. If you lose your balance, hold a wall or object and only lift one arm on one side at a time.

Be patient with yourself, since each step of the exercise asks something new of your body. It is better to start slowly, rather than rush and train undesirable or compensating muscle patterns. A common error is for people to shift their weight back as they reach the second leg back. This places your weight in "no-man's land" in the midair and causes you to lose your balance. Training your body to be very aware of which leg you are on, and where your body mass is, is very useful for learning better feel for horses under you. If you are unaware whether you are shifting your weight off the front leg, use a mirror or have someone observe you.

DEEP STRETCHING

Spend some extra time in one stretch each day for your tightest areas. Select from the Standard Warm-Up Stretches (p. 67), or others, and commit to holding the stretch for 2 to 3 minutes, a couple of times. Be patient and do not pull yourself into the stretch too deeply or too quickly.

STAMINA & COORDINATION

The cardio exercises are included in the *Warm-Up* for this week (see p. 83).

Week Three

Theme: Continue to build on the core base while integrating the core into movement and training symmetry.

Equipment Needed: Exercise ball, hand weights, exercise mat (special needs only), balance board (advanced only).

WARM-UP

Now that you are very familiar with the Standard Warm-Up Stretches, you are ready to speed it up a little!

1 | Warm up this week is 5 minutes by alternating between a cardiovascular interval to elevate your heart rate and one round of moving through all the Standard Warm-Up Stretches (p. 67).

2 | For the cardio interval, pick a favorite song to motivate you and "work it" rigorously for one minute. You can choose any activity that matches your circumstances: marching on the spot, kickboxing moves, jogging, or using exercise equipment.

WEEK THREE AT-A-GLANCE	
Warm-Up	Alternate 5 minutes elevated cardio with one round of dynamic Warm-Up Stretches.
Core Training	Ball Crunches with Isometric and Over-head Reaches, followed by the Plank. Do two sets.
Strength & Muscle Memory	Forward Raise Lying on Ball; Lateral Raise Seated on Ball.
Deep Stretching	Select a different area than Week Two for extra stretching. Hold your deep stretches for at least 3 minutes. Wall-Assisted Pectoral Stretches.
Stamina & Coordination	Build body coordination through Single Leg Squats with Arm Movements.
Special Needs Modifications	Forward Raise Lying on Floor.
Advanced Variations	Lateral Raise on Balance Board instead of seated; Single Leg Squats with upper body movement instead of just arm movement.
Notes	Riders with especially locked shoulders or tight chest muscles should be focusing on deep stretching for the chest and shoulders.

CORE TRAINING

Core exercises this week build on your ability for holding a neutral spine in spite of asymmetric loading or destabilizing surface. The core is also integrated into movement, by being a non-focus part of other exercises this week.

Ball Crunches with Isometric Overhead Reach

Goal: 10–12 reps.

Muscles Worked: Rectus abdominis, transverse abdominis, obliques, latissimus dorsi.

● ● ●

9.1 A–C
Ball Crunches with Isometric Overhead Reach.

1 | Perform a regular Ball Crunch, holding a weight at your belly with both hands (fig. 9.1 A).

2 | When you are at the top of the movement in the crunch, slowly and rhythmically reach the weight overhead until you feel that your *abdominals* are working very hard to retain your position (figs. 9.1 B & C).

3 | Return the weight to its starting position at your belly.

4 | Return your body to the relaxed position prior to performing the crunch.

5 | Take a deep breath. Repeat until fatigued.

Do not keep doing the exercise once you can no longer strongly support your spine by maintaining good position. As soon as you feel a tendency for your body to "sit down," or you feel some strain in your lower back, you have reached the point where your deep supportive muscles are fatigued and your set is finished.

The Plank—On Hands or Elbows

Goal: Hold for 30–60 seconds.

Muscles Worked: Obliques, deltoids, shoulder rotators, transverse abdominis, lower back area, pectorals, triceps.

To do the Plank properly, you need to use the feeling you have developed for tucking in your pelvis (see Floor Crunches, p. 78). Also, draw your stomach muscles upward with a feeling that you are making as much distance from the top of your head to your heels as possible. This exercise will help you build deep core strength.

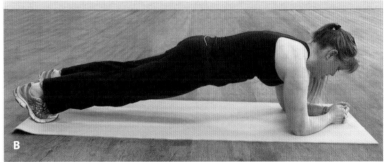

9.2 A & B The Plank—On Hands or Elbows.

● ● ●

1 | Start by positioning yourself on all fours on the floor as if about to do the Bird Dog exercises (p. 83).

2 | Lift your body up into a Plank position (fig. 9.2 A).

3 | Make sure that you lift your seat only very slightly, tucking your tailbone down, and pulling your pubic bone toward your ribs.

4 | Use a mirror or a partner to verify that your hips are level and you have good alignment from heel through hip to shoulder.

5 | Hold for as long as you can until you feel your back hollowing, then stop.

You can also do the Plank on your elbows, if you cannot do it with straight arms (fig. 9.2 B).

STRENGTH & MUSCLE MEMORY

Forward Raise Lying on Ball

Goal: 15 reps.

Muscles Worked: Erector spinae, transverse abdominis, upper gluteus maximus, lower trapezius, deltoids.

The appropriate weight size to use is the one that allows you to perform the 15 repetitions but also causes you to "fight" for your last few reps. If you have weak shoulders or a weak back, you may find you need to start out without any weight at all.

1 | Lie on the ball on your stomach, holding two weights (fig. 9.3 A).

2 | Position your arms beside you so that they fall around the ball toward the ground (hugging the ball).

3 | Looking forward, engage your stomach and back muscles, and lift your shoulders a little.

4 | Raise both arms slowly until they are ahead of you and parallel to the floor. Hold for a second and slowly return them to the start position (fig. 9.3 B).

Generally, a rhythmical count of 3 to 4 can be used for the lift, and again for the return to start of most exercises. Performing the exercises rhythmically helps your muscles learn faster, ensures you are not compensating, and builds more endurance.

Special Needs Modification
Forward Raise Lying on Floor

Goal: 10–12 reps.

Muscles Worked: Erector spinae, lower trapezius, deltoids, transverse abdominis, light use of gluteals.

This exercise is really a modification of the Bird Dog exercises (p. 83) or the Superman exercise (p. 160). The Forward Raise Lying on Ball can

●●●

9.3 A & B Forward Raise Lying on Ball.

9.4 Forward Raise Lying on Floor.

be modified to a Forward Raise Lying on Floor for more back support, or done with bent elbows if you have a shoulder impingement. Mobility can be improved in shoulders through a chest stretch, using the wall as your assistant.

Lying on the floor instead of a ball removes the element of instability; to keep the balance benefit (if you can), lie with a cushion under your stomach/pelvis area.

1 | Stretch your body into a long position with arms in front of you, holding light weights (fig. 9.4). If you have impinged shoulders or very weak shoulders, you can start with no weights, or with arms bent so your elbows are at 90 degrees (your forearms will be beside your head and not in front of you).

2 | Take a breath and engage your core muscles, then lift the weights as well as your chest and head.

The range of movement you are able to achieve is not as important as the fact that you engage your back and shoulder muscles together, and symmetrically.

Lateral Raise Seated on Ball

Goal: 10–12 reps.

Muscles Worked: Deltoids, light engagement of transverse abdominis and obliques to prevent ball wobble.

This exercise helps you maintain stability and straightness through your core while tempting your body to tilt at the shoulders. At the same time, you will also be building some shoulder strength, which is very useful for preventing injury working with and around horses.

To do this exercise, you need to engage your *transverse abdominis,* the deep abdominal muscle encircling your waist, which was worked through the Plank (p. 95). Don't think too hard about it. Envisioning this muscle squeezing in like a girdle should be sufficient. Also, imagine there is a cable between your pubic bone and bottom ribs, and you are attaching it. This will help you maintain correct ribcage position and spine alignment, and help prevent the tendency to throw the shoulders back and stiffen the upper back.

1 | Sit on your exercise ball with a neutral spine—that is, with the feeling there is a string pulling your head to the ceiling and engaged abdominals (not slouching but not stiff).

Dangle your arms beside you, holding weights (fig. 9.5 A).

2 | Purposefully engage your *transverse abdominis* and push your shoulders and arms down.

3 | Lift your arms to shoulder height, in alignment with your shoulder girdle, while maintaining a feeling of pressing your shoulders down. Pressing your shoulders down while lifting the arms will keep your *trapezius* muscle from cheating and engaging, and keep the exercise focused on the *deltoids* going over your shoulder socket. If you need to, practice the movement first one arm at a time to make sure that the powerful *trapezius* muscle is not doing all the lifting (figs. 9.5 B–D).

9.5 A–D
Lateral Raise
Seated on Ball.

● ● ●

Advanced Variation

Lateral Raise on Balance Board

Goal: 15 reps.

Muscles Worked: Deltoids, transverse abdominis, erector spinae, stabilizers in hip, knee and ankle, gluteals, hamstring, quadriceps.

This exercise works the shoulders and integrates your core by requiring your body to combine spine stabilization and correct postures at each phase of the movement. By standing on a balance board instead of sitting on a ball, you are increasing the level of instability that your body has to cope with in order to keep your shoulders level. You are also increasing the amount of body coordination required since your brain now has to work with soft lower-body joints, a toned core, plus correct technique in the lift. For this exercise, do not use a "wobble board" (constantly unstable). You only need lateral (side-to-side) instability for this exercise, and you need to be able to achieve a neutral position.

1 │ Start by standing on the balance board (or board over a pool noodle or rolled up towel) in the athletic-ready and neutral stance. Hold weights in your hands.

2 │ Push your hands and shoulders downward, then lift the weights to shoulder height while maintaining a feeling of pushing the shoulders down. Lift rhythmically up and down,

9.6 A & B
Lateral Raise on Balance Board.

● ● ●

breathing on the *down* phase, and engaging your core on the *up* phase (figs. 9.6 A & B).

If you wobble on the board or lose your balance, restore your balance and stability before proceeding.

DEEP STRETCHING

Select a different area than the one you focused on in Week Two for extra stretching. Use any of the stretches already introduced that target your new area. By this time in the workout, the exercises will have helped you identify your tight areas that need the most work (they will be impeding your ability to do the exercises, or do them symmetrically).

Stay consistent for the week in focusing on this one area. Hold your stretches for at least 3 to 6 minutes. It is okay to push the envelope a little by asking for more of a stretch. Also you can "pause" the stretching in order to shake out the area whenever it gets too intense.

●●●

9.7 A & B Wall-Assisted Pectoral Stretch.

Wall-Assisted Pectoral Stretch

Goal: 15–60 seconds hold on each side. Repeat twice.

Muscles Worked: Pectorals (chest area) and shoulder rotators.

This exercise makes use of a wall and moving your body to achieve more chest and shoulder stretch.

1 | Stand beside a wall so that it is at your side, in a straight or split-leg position.

2 | Place your hand on the wall even with or above your head if your shoulder will allow (fig. 9.7 A).

3 | Once your hand is pressing on the wall, crouch down and walk your body forward slightly, leaving your hand in its original position (fig. 9.7 B).

You can use your legs to support your weight and to control how long you remain in the stretch and how far you go. As with all stretches, you should only feel it as a "3" to "5" out of "10" on a scale of discomfort at first. With relaxation and breathing, the sense of the stretch should decrease. When it does, you know that the muscle fibers are lengthening and you are relaxing. If the degree of the stretch feeling does not reduce, ease up to give your body a chance to relax into it.

STAMINA & COORDINATION

Cardio time is reduced a little this week to leave more time for the coordination exercises. The Single Leg Squats will build body coordination and also strengthen the *hip stabilizers* (muscles around the hip sockets).

Single Leg Squats with Arm Movements

Goal: 6 reps (left and right equals one rep).

Muscles Worked: Gluteus maximus, medius and minimus, quadriceps, hamstrings, small ankle and knee stabilizing ligaments and muscles, deltoids, erector spinae, transverse abdominis.

1 | Adopt the athletic neutral stance (legs shoulder-width, knees slightly bent, spine neutral, neck soft, abs engaged).

2 | Shift your weight to one foot and lift the other slightly off the ground. Your seat bones should be pointing backward somewhat, and knees, ankles, and hip joints soft, but very stable.

3 | Once all of your weight is on one leg, sit a little deeper into the squat. Only go as far as you can without wobbling. Make sure that your seat pokes back and your knee

9.8 Single Leg Squats with Arm Movements.

● ● ●

stays behind your toes. It is a common error for people to allow the knee to drive forward, which only puts negative pressure on the knee while disengaging the hip muscles.

4 | Once you are in the squat position and stable, slowly move your arms around in different positions for a few seconds: first individually, then both at once (fig. 9.8).

5 | Stand up, return to neutral, shift to the other leg, and repeat.

9.9 A & B
Single Leg
Squats with
Upper Body
Rotations.

Single Leg Squats with Upper Body Rotations

Goal: 10 reps (left and right equals one rep).

Muscles Worked: Gluteals, hamstrings, quadriceps, stabilizers in knee, hip, and ankle, transverse abdominis, obliques.

This exercise works strength, balance, core control, and coordination, all at once.

1 | Perform the Single Leg Squats as instructed on p. 101.

2 | Once your balance is stable, introduce instability and challenge coordination by twisting or moving your torso in different directions, while maintaining stability in the hips and leg (figs. 9.9 A & B).

If you start to tire before you have completed the set, scale back to using just arm movements, or not sitting so deeply into the squat, in order to complete the set.

Week Four

Theme: Building lateral stability and leg movement accuracy.

Equipment Needed: Exercise mat, access to a stair or stool, exercise ball or light object, exercise tubing or band (Advanced Variation only).

Introduction: Be patient and accurate with this week's exercises. They may seem simple, but the task of teaching your body to integrate your core and stabilize your spine while performing tasks against resistance in different planes is a foundation to later training. Without this basic ability, you place yourself at risk of straining your back when doing more intensive exercise. What you learn this week will also help you with better ergonomics for working around the horses and farm.

For all of this week's exercises, your back should be straight and your core engaged—don't let your lower back collapse.

WEEK FOUR AT-A-GLANCE	
Warm-Up	Cycle through the Standard Warm-Up Stretches once, march on the spot or do stairs for 2 minutes, then cycle through the Warm-Up Stretches a second time.
Core Training	Bicycle Crunches; Side Plank; Standing "Round the World."
Strength & Muscle Memory	Side Lying Leg Lifts.
Deep Stretching	Hip Rotator Stretch; Calf Stretch; Deep Chest Stretch. You target deep stretches for calves, chest, and hamstrings (Lying Hamstring Stretch from Week One).
Stamina & Coordination	Move through your exercise routine briskly to elevate heartrate. Bonus if you can do 2–3, 10-minute-long additional brisk walks or jogs.
Special Needs Modifications	Modified versions of Bicycle Crunches, the Side Plank, and Standing "Round the World" with Torso.
Advanced Variations	Add resistance to Standing Side Leg Lifts and Push, and Standing "Round the World," by using exercise tubing.
Notes	Keep your back straight (neutral) and core engaged through all exercises.

WARM-UP

The warm-up this week is shorter to leave room for learning the other exercises. Cycle through the Standard Warm-Up Stretches, march on the spot, or do stairs for 2 minutes, then cycle through the Standard Warm-Up Stretches a second time.

CORE TRAINING

These core exercises teach *proprioception* (awareness of where your body is) while building core strength all around your torso. They also build thigh strength as you maintain a solid stance in your legs and hips. Since core and other muscles are integrated this week, both the Core Training and the Strength & Stability exercises will train thigh and core muscles at the same time. The act of integrating them teaches your body to engage the core for leg movement and stability.

Bicycle Crunches

Goal: 20 reps (left and right equals one rep).

Muscles Worked: Rectus abdominis, transverse abdominis, obliques, hip flexors (psoas), lower back and lower abdominal area.

Bicycle Crunches work on cross-body coordination and the core muscle connections that help stabilize hips and shoulders, while also challenging your lower back/low *abdominals* because of the added loading from the weight of your extended leg.

1 | Lie on the floor as if you are about to do a sit-up, with your hands behind your head and neck.

2 | Lift one leg toward you, knee bent, until your lower leg is parallel with the ground.

3 | As you lift your leg, lift your upper body into a basic crunch position then reach across your

● ● ●

10.1 A & B Bicycle Crunches.

body with your shoulder/armpit. Imagine you are trying to reach the outside of the opposite knee (fig. 10.1 A).

4 | Return your torso and leg to the neutral start position, and repeat on the other side (fig. 10.1 B).

Common errors are doing them too fast or not extending the straight leg enough. Do them slowly, counting your repetitions in pairs (left and right equals one rep). Maintain your back position on the floor, and be aware that the minute you can no longer keep your back from hollowing, you need to stop the exercise and rest before completing your 20 reps. Ignoring technique by going too quickly at first will work against your core-training goals.

Special Needs Modification
Bicycle Crunches— Legs Higher

Goal: 10–12 reps.

Having your legs parallel with the ground puts a lot of pressure on your lower back. This pressure forces your lower back muscles to strengthen. However, if you are particularly weak in the lower back or stomach, the pressure will be negative. To adapt the exercise, "bicycle" your legs higher up in the air (figs. 10.2 A & B). This will reduce the need for your lower *abdominals* and lower back muscles to support your leg weight.

10.2 A & B Bicyle Crunches—Legs Higher.

● ● ●

Side Plank

Goal: 60 seconds each side.

Muscles Worked: Transverse abdominis, hip stabilizers and gluteus medius, obliques, shoulder rotators, triceps.

The Side Plank is all about alignment and building lateral postural stamina.

1 | Lie on one side. Line your body up shoulder to hip to knee with a feeling of *abdominals* engagement.

2 | Extend the arm under your body straight down below your shoulder, lifting your hips off the floor, and extending the opposite arm straight up in the air, holding the position (figs. 10.3 A & B). If you find the Side Plank difficult to do, just hold for a few seconds, rest, then repeat until you have accumulated 30 seconds.

10.3 A & B
Side Plank.

● ● ●

Lateral strengthening exercises like this are so beneficial to riders because they are often forgotten. Riders are aware of forward and back motion of riding; however, because they do not frequently stick their legs out to the side, they tend to forget that lateral strength is also important.

Just as with horses, the human body is better supported in forward movement by lateral strength. Also, the horse depends on the rider providing clear and solid lateral support—not to physically muscle the horse, but to guide him consistently. When a rider is weak laterally, she loses effectiveness in her aids and control of the horse's balance.

Special Needs Modification
Side Plank on Elbow, Knees, and Object

Goal: 20–30 seconds each side.

If you are unable to perform a full Side Plank, you can adapt the exercise while still getting benefit for your core by doing the exercise on your elbows, your knees, or with a shallower incline propped up on an object such as the arm of your couch or a step stool (figs. 10.4 A–C). Gradually, you will increase the time you can hold the exercise before a rest.

10.4 A–C Side Plank on Elbow, Knees, and Object.

● ● ●

10.5 A & B
Standing
"Round the
World" with
Torso.

●●●

Standing "Round the World" with Torso

Goal: 6–8 complete circuits.

Muscles Worked: Obliques, erector spinae, transverse abdominis, deltoids.

This exercise is mostly for your outer core muscles that lift and move your torso. It is secondarily beneficial to your shoulder muscles. The amount of weight you carry and the degree to which your arms are raised will be limited by your shoulder strength and degree of ability for rotation in your shoulders. Do not compromise spine alignment for the sake of lifting your arms higher or carrying more weight.

1 | Stand in athletic neutral stance holding a fitness ball or weight in front of your body, then bringing it overhead, arms extended. Make sure that your core is engaged, and spine neutral with knees bent (fig. 10.5 A & B).

2 | Tip sideways while keeping your spine neutral, only as far as you can tip while still being able to control the movement with your *obliques* (fig. 10.5 C).

3 | Engage your *abdominals* and pull your torso back to neutral with your obliques.

4 | Work your way around a semi-circle: tip forward, then to the other side (fig. 10.5 D).

5 | Work your way back in the other direction.

10.5 C & D
Standing "Round the World" with Torso.

● ● ●

6 | If your arms or shoulders tire before your core does, put down the object or lower your arms.

Special Needs Modification
Standing "Round the World" with Bent Elbows

If you have a shoulder impingement, weaker shoulders, or back issues, the "Round the World" exercise can be modified to reduce loading to your lower back and shoulders in two main ways. Either do the exercise without weight, or bend your arms when holding the object above your head and at chest or belly level (figs. 10.6 A & B).

10.6 A & B Standing "Round the World" with Bent Elbows.

● ● ●

STRENGTH & MUSCLE MEMORY

Side Lying Leg Lifts

Goal: 20 reps on each side.

Muscles Worked: Transverse abdominis, obliques, gluteus medius and minimus, Iliotibial (IT) band.

10.7 A & B
Side Lying
Leg Lifts.

● ● ●

Posture is very important with this exercise, since the workout comes from the act of keeping your shoulder-hip-heel alignment, while moving your thigh against resistance— just as you need to do when riding.

1 │ Lie on the ground with your knees bent, and alignment in shoulder, hip, and ankle. You will need to engage your stomach muscles.

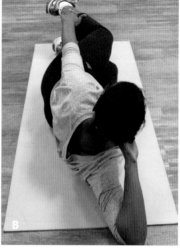

2 │ Reach your hand over your hip and toward your ankle as you raise your leg, lower, and repeat (figs. 10.7 A & B).

Be careful! It is easy to cheat by turning your toe toward the ceiling and using your hip flexors to lift your leg instead. The goal of this exercise is not to lift the leg very high, but to

isolate the muscles on the outside of your hip and leg. Keep your foot parallel with the floor.

Advanced Variation
Side Leg Lift with Resistance

Goal: 20–30 reps.

To add some challenge to this exercise, loop an exercise band or tube around your feet to increase the resistance (fig. 10.8). Adding resistance makes it harder to maintain correct alignment. You can also try ankle weights.

10.8 Side Leg Lift with Resistance.

● ● ●

Advanced Variation
Standing Side Leg Push with Resistance

Goal: 20–30 reps (left and right equals one rep).

This additional Advanced Variation involves shifting your posture from horizontal to upright. When you are upright, you will not be able to rely on the floor to keep your torso straight. You have to rely on muscle memory for a spine neutral posture, and on core strength to provide a base from which your thigh pushes outward.

1 | Stand in spine-neutral position with your core engaged, and exercise tubing looped around your feet.

2 | Shift your weight to one side so that you can lift your other leg (fig. 10.9 A).

3 | Push your free leg outward against the resistance of the band (fig. 10.9 B).

4 | Return the leg to the neutral standing position (feet about 2 feet apart, or the width of a yoga mat), and immediately perform the exercise on the other side. Go back and forth, left and right.

Be careful not to let the exercise tubing pull your feet in close together. Keeping them out at all times is what is providing the exercise for your thighs. Also, be careful to

10.9 A & B Standing Side Leg Push with Resistance.

● ● ●

remain upright with good posture in your torso and core muscles engaged. Do not allow your upper body to "tick-tock" side to side. Keeping your torso upright will train your body to stabilize through the core.

When a rider is weak in the muscle areas targeted by this exercise, she often unconsciously cheats by performing movement with the upper body instead. To stop from doing this, watch yourself in a mirror. Doing it correctly requires coordination and core integration. Start out slowly to make sure you can do it without moving your upper body about or losing straightness and alignment in your hips.

DEEP STRETCHING

Hip Rotator Stretch

Goal: To achieve relaxation on both sides before giving.

Muscles Worked: Piriformis, gluteals, hip rotators, iliotibial band (IT band).

This stretch targets the *piriformis* and the muscle chain going from your *gluteals* to your knee.

1 | Lie on the mat as if you were about to perform a Floor Crunch.

2 | Place your right ankle on the left knee. See if you can get your legs to be at right angles to one another by pushing your right knee outward.

3 | Lift your left foot off the floor to use your left thigh to bring both of your legs closer to your chest.

4 | Reach through the space in the middle of your legs to hold onto your left thigh. Use your arms to gently pull your legs a little closer to your chest (fig. 10.10).

5 | Repeat with the other leg.

Depending how tight your hips are, you may not be able to get deeply into this stretch. Take your time. If you are very tight, this stretch will reveal a lot of tightness in your hips and help you to mobilize them. If you feel pain in the knee, it means that your hips are so tight they are not moving, and your knee is giving in too much in order for your body to achieve the posture. Ease up. You do not want to strain your knee. You want your hip to slowly loosen.

● ● ●

10.10 Hip Rotator Stretch.

Calf Stretch

Goal: Continue until you feel a lengthening of your leg, about 30–60 seconds.

Muscles Worked: *Calf muscles (gastrocnesmius and soleus) and Achilles tendon.*

To do this stretch correctly, your stretching leg has to be fully relaxed, which means that it cannot be supporting your weight.

1 | Stand with both feet firmly on a stair or object.

2 | Shift your weight completely onto one foot.

3 | Shift the free foot so that the ball of your foot is on the edge of the step and you can reach your heel downward (fig. 10.11).

4 | Stretch your heel down until you can feel the stretch on a scale of "3" to "4" out of "10."

5 | Use deep breathing to slowly relax your leg muscles (about 20 to 30 seconds), reaching your heel farther down only when you feel relaxation in the area.

10.11 Calf Stretch.

● ● ●

Be careful to keep your toes pointing directly forward. Many people who are particularly tight in the calf or ankle will cheat by turning their toe out. To get at the problem area, you need to align your foot so that the stretch targets a line directly behind your heel and knee.

Deep Chest Stretch

Goal: Continue until your chest muscles relax, about 30–90 seconds.

Muscles Worked: Pectorals, shoulder rotators.

This stretch targets the *pectoralis major* and *minor*, as well as some *shoulder rotators* and the line stretching into your bicep. These are the muscles that pull a chest forward and down, and block a rider from having a correct but relaxed shoulder position.

1 | Start by placing your hand on a wall or fence post level with your shoulder, palm forward facing.

2 | Walk forward a step or two, keeping your hand in place so that your arm is straight and you begin to feel a stretch across the chest (fig. 10.12).

3 | When the stretch is a "3" to "4" out of "10," hold that position and breathe deeply until you feel a giving and relaxation in the area.

4 | Walk a little farther forward to increase the stretch again.

5 | Change the position of your hand so that it is a little higher up, and repeat.

The maximum height you should reach for is directly over your head. If you are very tight, walk into the stretch, breathe, then ease up. Then, walk into it again.

10.12 Deep Chest Stretch.

● ● ●

STAMINA & COORDINATION

To maintain cardiovascular fitness and improve muscle coordination, the goal this week is to hit a groove with your exercise routine fairly early on so you can cycle through all the exercises 2 or 3 times at a steady, heart-elevating pace (without rushing). Move from one exercise to the other as much as possible, without breaks. If you are able, fit in a few 10-minute sessions of very brisk walking.

Week Five

Theme: Combining movements to increase proprioception while integrating core stability (your ability to maintain a stable core or neutral spine by integrating core engagement into your exercises).

Equipment Needed: Exercise ball, hand weight, balance board, glasses of water.

Introduction: This week's workout consists of a regular training session, with added options you can select, depending on the discipline you ride. These *Discipline Variations* are not divided by saddle type but are grouped by the type of demand made on *your* body. The goal is to train the basic body movement and conditioning skills needed for you to perform. From a human conditioning point of view, it is more meaningful to organize training by physical demand. The key differentiating factors to riding disciplines include duration of time, need for intense bursts of effort, and the use of aids primarily

WEEK FIVE AT-A-GLANCE	
Warm-Up	Do a 6-minute warm-up in which you alternate between 1 minute of heart-rate elevating exercise, and 1 minute of flowing stretches, using the Standard Warm-Up Stretches.
Core Training	Ball Pass; Back Extensions; Leg Lowers; and Side Plank with Aligned Leg Lift.
Strength & Muscle Memory	Overhead Pass Seated with Weight and with One Foot Raised.
Deep Stretching	Return to a focus on your chest muscles and shoulder mobility, using stretches from the Standard Warm-Up or a previous week. Pick 1 or 2 stretches to use daily for at least 1–2 minutes each.
Stamina & Coordination	Cardiovascular requirement is included in the warm-up.
Special Needs Modifications	Modified Ball Pass; Leg Lowers; Side Plank with Minor Leg Lift; Overhead Pass; and Overhead Pass—Seated *without* Weight.
Advanced Variations	Side Plank with Full Leg Lift.
Discipline: Intense	10 minutes of intensity intervals: 30-second burst alternating with 60 seconds recovery (but still moving).
Discipline: Raised Seat	Ride Gymnastic Holding Water Glasses twice a week, 5 minutes each time.
Discipline: Seated	Stand on Balance Board and Multitask 3 times weekly, 3–5 minutes.
Notes	The goal this week is to get used to splitting your workout into manageable chunks as you add in your discipline stream.

through pelvis and seat as opposed to leg and hand contact. The three main groupings are:

Intense: This group describes the riding disciplines in which intensive bursts of effort are required, placing large demand on the heart in brief spurts, combined with a significant repetition of this demand sustained over time. Examples are Western sports such as barrel racing and roping, and mounted games, polo, and eventing. Other riders whose sports place similar demands on them should follow this training track.

Raised Seat: This group describes the disciplines in which the rider has primary contact with the horse's body through the legs, and experiences demand intervals over a relatively short period of time. Examples include hunters and jumpers.

Seated: The rider's *main* contact and control mechanism with her horse are her seat bones and pelvis, rather than hands and legs. (Hands, arm position, and upper and lower leg are all secondary to the primary guiding mechanism, which is the seat. This is illustrated nicely by riders who demonstrate high-level movements without a bridle and para-athletes.) The ride does not require the same cardiovascular fitness as a riding style that includes intervals and bursts of high intensity. Also, there are different leg- and seat-muscle patterns than for the raised-seat disciplines. However, subtlety, coordination, core control, and sufficient cardiovascular fitness to sustain effort over time are important. Examples include reining, Western pleasure, and dressage.

For the remainder of this entire workout plan, *Discipline Variation* exercises will be added for each of these three training-requirement categories. These new exercises will be shown at the end of the week's basic training plan.

While it does not matter which track you choose, it does matter that you choose one and stick with it for the remainder of the workout series. The exercises in each discipline stream build on one another from week to week in a progressive manner. Constantly switching between discipline categories would be as confusing to your body as constantly switching the discipline you are training would be to your horse, and to his conditioning. Stick with one discipline track from Week Five through to Week Nine. If you practice several riding styles or want to challenge yourself differently when you have completed the nine weeks, come back

Demand Intervals

These are intervals or spurts of time in which the body experiences a physical demand higher than the average for that workout. A rider's heart-rate monitor usually shows when these moments are, since the heart rate is often elevated. Even when it is not, there is either a momentary increased need for oxygen or muscle exertion.

to Week Five and repeat Weeks Five through Nine following a different discipline track.

(See p. 126 for Week Five's *Discipline Variations*.)

> *The goal is to elevate your heart rate for short segments, then release tension from your body by using one round of the Standard Warm-Up exercises."*

WARM-UP

Do a 6-minute warm-up in which you alternate 1 minute of heart-rate elevating exercise (any type that suits you and your available equipment) and 1 minute of flowing stretches using the Standard Warm-Up Stretch routine. The goal is to elevate your heart rate for short segments, then release tension from your body by using one round of the Standard Warm-Up exercises. Since this is a dynamic stretch routine, it can also be used between intense exercises (or between rides) to momentarily loosen yourself up again or work out areas that have become tense—without overstretching them.

CORE TRAINING

The core workout this week is a very efficient series of exercises that cover *upper and lower abdominals, back,* and *sides*.

Ball Pass

Goal: 20 repetitions, 2 sets.

Muscles Worked: Rectus abdominis, hip flexors (psoas) adductors, lower back area, light work of latissimus dorsi, and triceps.

This exercise will use your upper, middle, and lower *abdominals* while getting you to coordinate different movements in your upper and lower body. It will also work your lower back.

1 | Lie on the floor as if you were going to do a Floor Crunch, knees slightly bent with your arms overhead, resting on the ground. Hold the ball between your hands or feet (fig. 11.1 A).

2 | Lift your legs straight up and lift your arms at the same time, crunching up off the floor—shoulder blades and head off the floor (fig. 11.1 B).

3 | "Pass" the ball from feet to hands, and vice-versa (fig. 11.1 C).

4 | Lower your arms and legs down again to the starting position (fig. 11.1 D). Repeat.

11.1 A–D Ball Pass.

● ● ●

Raising and lowering the ball with your legs is a lot of work for your lower abdominals and lower back. If you feel that you are beginning to no longer keep your lower back pressed onto the floor, then reduce the pressure by either not lowering your legs as far, or by bending your knees. The motion of passing the ball also works your *groin* area and *adductor* muscles, which really helps with inner-thigh strength for riding.

Special Needs Modification
Modified Ball Pass

Goal: 10 reps, 2 sets.

Perform the Ball Pass exercise but do not lower either your arms or your legs all the way to the floor.

1 │ Start in a more curled/crunched position.

2 │ Raise your arms and the ball and your legs above you to perform the pass, while performing a crunch with your abdominals.

3 │ When you have transitioned the ball between hands and legs, lower your limbs only a few feet before exchanging the ball again. If you need to rest, simply lower everything to the ground and give yourself a moment to recover before continuing until you have completed the set.

Back Extensions

Goal: 20–30 reps, 2 sets.

Muscles Worked: Erector spinae, transverse abdominis, gluteus maximus, hamstrings (depending on leg position), lower trapezius (depending on arm position).

This exercise works your back from one end to the other. Performing the exercise on a fitness ball forces you to self-monitor symmetry, since you will have to use even strength on both sides to keep the ball stable.

1 | Start by lying over the ball, so that the ball is under your pelvis, not only your belly (if the ball is in the right position, you can't stay on it without hooking your feet under something, or against the wall). The exercise is much harder with your feet held by a partner, against the corner of the wall and floor, or under an object, but you can do mini-back extensions even if you have nowhere to hook your feet (figs. 11.2 A & B).

2 | With your hands placed behind your head, lift your torso until it is in alignment with your legs. Lifting your back too high will place negative pressure on your lower back (figs. 11.2 C & D).

3 | To add difficulty, repeat several times and then hold yourself up for several seconds.

This is a foundational exercise for the lower-back muscles. Most riders with weak lower *abdominals* also have weak lower-back muscles and a very hard (or painful) time maintaining correct back posture.

11.2 A–D Back Extensions.

● ● ●

Leg Lowers

Goal: 30 reps.

Muscles Worked: Hip flexors, lower abdominal (mostly lower rectus abdominis) and lower back area, transverse abdominis.

This exercise looks like a leg *lift* in the photos. A leg *lift* recruits the *hip flexors* (*psoas*) muscles to lift your legs in the air. Since riders tend to get tight in the hip flexors (including *psoas*), it is better for riders to do leg *lowers*. Lowering the legs instead of lifting them

●●●
11.3 A–E Leg Lowers.

helps to focus the exercise on the lower back and lower *abdominals.*

1 | Lie on your back as if about to do a crunch (fig. 11.3 A).

2 | Bend your knees, pull in your legs then straighten them into the air (fig. 11.3 B).

3 | Keeping your back pressing on the floor, slowly lower your legs to about one-third, or until you feel increased difficulty in keeping your lower back pressing onto the floor (figs. 11.3 C & D).

4 | Hold for 3 seconds, then bend your knees, put your feet down, and repeat (fig. 11.3 E).

Modified Leg Lowers

Goal: 15–30 each side.

The Leg Lowers exercise can be modified by doing only one leg at a time, or lowering your legs only a couple of inches (figs. 11.4 A–D).

11.4 A–D Modified Leg Lowers.

11.5 Side Plank with Aligned Leg Lift.

● ● ●

Side Plank with Aligned Leg Lift

Goal: 12–20 on each side, 2 sets.

Muscles Worked: Transverse abdominis, obliques, shoulder rotators and triceps, gluteus medius and minimus, hip stabilizers.

This is a variation of the Side Plank (p. 106), with the added demand or loading created by shifting your leg weight.

1 | Lie on your side on the floor, then prop yourself up on your elbow, or your hand. I like to keep one arm extended above me for balance, or you can tuck it behind your back as shown in the picture.

2 | Pick your hips up off the mat so they are in alignment between your shoulders and feet; you will need to really push the bottom edge of your bottom foot away from you.

3 | Lift your top leg as high as you can while maintaining your balance and alignment (fig. 11.5).

4 | Hold the plank position while lifting your leg up and down to perform the repetitions.

You will feel this exercise the most on the side closest to the floor. Riders often develop a strength imbalance between their inner and outer thigh, and this is an excellent corrective exercise with this in mind.

Special Needs Modification
Side Plank on an Incline with Minor Leg Lift

Goal: 10–12 reps.

1 | Perform a Side Plank according to your ability either on an incline (object), knees, or elbows (fig. 11.6).

2 | Raise your leg only a few inches, either straight, or bent, according to your ability.

11.6 Side Plank with Minor Leg Lift.

● ● ●

Advanced Variation
Side Plank on Hand with Full Leg Lift

Goal: 15–20 reps each side, 2 sets.

1 | Perform a full Side Plank up on your hand.

2 | Raise your leg as high as you can without compromising torso alignment or stability in your plank, and keeping your foot parallel to the ground (fig. 11.7).

3 | Introduce an even *more* Advanced Variation by raising your leg, then shifting its position (forward, backward, or circles) while maintaining stability in your body.

11.7 Side Plank on Hand with Full Leg Lift.

● ● ●

Note: If your core is ready for this variation *but* your wrist or shoulder muscles are not, you can modify the exercise by performing the Plank on your elbow on the mat, or with your elbow on a soft surface such as a cushion, arm of a couch, or a fitness ball.

STRENGTH & MUSCLE MEMORY

The strength exercises this week train you to simultaneously use your core for torso stability while performing movement variations with asymmetrical demand.

Overhead Pass—Seated with Weight

Goal: 15–20 reps.

Muscles Worked: Transverse abdominis, obliques, deltoids.

1 | Start by sitting on your fitness ball in a spine-neutral posture, legs a little apart, even seat bone contact with the ball, and core engaged, but without tension in your shoulders. Grasp a weighted object in one hand.

2 | Raise both arms up to the side, then up overhead. Maintain alignment across your shoulder girdle and pay attention to your spine posture so that you do not lean back. You also should not have tension in your shoulders and neck. Keep your *abdominals* engaged and a sense of pushing your shoulders down while raising your arms (figs. 11.8 A–C).

3 | Exchange the object between your hands overhead (fig. 11.8 D).

4 | Slowly lower your arms to the neutral position, hanging beside you (fig. 11.8 E).

11.8 A–E
Overhead Pass–
Seated with
Weight.

●●●

Passing the object from *right* to *left* and *back again* is considered one repetition. Passing it in one direction only is only half of a repetition. The goal is to maintain straightness in both hips and shoulders, using your torso to resist the pressure to collapse or compensate. If you cannot lift the weight you are using without maintaining a straight torso, you are using too much weight.

Special Needs Modification
Overhead Pass—Seated without Weight

Goal: 15 reps.

Perform the Overhead Pass seated on the ball, but without weight in your hands (figs. 11.9 A–G). If you have a shoulder impingement, use bent elbows. As you do this exercise, position your arms overhead one at a time after you initially raise them to shoulder height. Being precise with your arm movements trains body awareness and coordination.

11.9 A–G Overhead Pass—Seated without Weight.

●●●

11.10 Overhead Pass with Leg Raised.

● ● ●

Overhead Pass with Leg Raised

Goal: 5 reps (full passes with each leg raised).

Muscles Worked: Same as Overhead Pass (see p. 124), but hip flexors (psoas) and quadriceps are added for the raised leg.

Perform the Overhead Pass exercise but with one foot raised slightly off the floor (fig. 11.10). You will need to place the remaining foot more centrally in front of you, and focus more on your balance. Complete 5 full passes with one leg raised, then switch legs for an additional 5 passes.

STAMINA & COORDINATION

Your cardio requirement was included in the warm-up this week as you adjust to adding in your *Discipline Variation* exercises.

DISCIPLINE VARIATIONS

Intense

Supplement this week's workout with cardiovascular training three times in the week (machines, running, elliptical, bike, swim). Go for 10 minutes as a minimum, using intervals the entire time: use a burst of effort as intense as you can for approximately 30 seconds, followed by slowing down for 60 seconds to recover. Repeat the cycle for 10 minutes. These very short cardio workouts can be done on consecutive days.

Raised Seat
"Ride" Gymnastics Holding Water Glasses

Goal: 2 times a week, 5 minutes each.

Focus: Coordination and integrated core stability.

1 | Start in a spine-neutral/athletic-neutral stance, holding two glasses of water (figs. 11.10 A & B).

2 | Visualize a jumping course or obstacle course and "ride" it.

3 | Coordinate breathing in order to have soft joints, while maintaining core stability, and adjust for raising and lowering your body without losing any water from the glasses.

4 | You can increase intensity by extending the length of time you do the exercise, or the amount you lower your body to build more leg strength, or by doing the exercise on a balance board.

If you need to work on your balance, you can begin this exercise by performing it on the balance board near a wall or object you can touch to balance yourself, while holding a glass of water in one hand only.

● ● ●

11.10 A & B
"Ride" Gymnastics
Holding Water
Glasses.

11.11 Multitasking on Balance Board.

● ● ●

Seated
Multitasking on Balance Board

Goal: 3 times a week for 3–5 minutes.

Focus: Softness through joints, good posture, and core stability.

1 | Start in a spine-neutral/athletic-neutral stance on the balance board with arms and body in riding position.

2 | Introduce asymmetrical movement by moving one arm around, then the other (fig. 11.11).

3 | Introduce further asymmetry and coordination by moving each arm in a different pattern, simultaneously.

4 | Return to neutral.

5 | Incorporate upper- and lower-body asymmetry by doing something with one foot, such as curling and uncurling your toes, or toe-tapping, while performing a different movement with your arm or hand.

chapter 12

Week Six

WEEK SIX AT-A-GLANCE	
Warm-Up	Two 4-minute cycles, containing 3 minutes of the new warm-up exercises (Standing Twists, Opposite Knee to elbow March, Furious Bicycle Crunches), and 1 minute of Standard Warm-Up Stretches.
Core Training	Weighted Side Bend on Ball; Ball Crunch with Curve; Ball Plank.
Strength & Muscle Memory	Deadlift with Weights; Single Leg Forward Tip.
Deep Stretching	Stretch a tight area, but also focus on hip mobility by alternatively doing long stretches using Hip Flexor to Ankle Stretch (Lunge and Press) and Hip Rotator Stretch.
Stamina & Coordination	Aim to increase cardiovascular capacity with the Standard Warm-Up rotation, then move through exercises with as few breaks as possible.
Special Needs Modifications	Deadlift without Weight; Single Leg Forward Tip with Balance Aid; Bicycle Crunch, Slower with Feet Higher in Air.
Advanced Variations	Deadlift on Balance Board; Single Leg Forward Tip Incorporating Arms and/or Weight.
Discipline: Intense	15–20 minute speed interval sessions using 3 minutes steadily increasing speed and 1 minute recovery; Squats.
Discipline: Raised Seat	Ride 2 imaginary courses, at different speeds, for 8–10 minutes, 2 times in week. Holding Water Glasses twice a week, 5 minutes.
Discipline: Seated	5–10 minutes of hip-mobilizing walk patterns, 3 times in week.
Notes	None.

Theme: Increasing cross-body coordination.

Equipment Needed: Exercise ball, exercise mat, hand weights, balance board.

Introduction: Now that you have the habit of fitting your exercises into your schedule, and you have a good base of core strength and coordination, you are ready to increase the general intensity of your workout and incorporate more full body movement.

WARM-UP

Do two 4-minute cycles consisting of 3 minutes of changing up the three exercises I'm about to describe, followed by 1 minute of Standard Warm-Up Stretches (p. 67).

Note: If you have high blood pressure or cannot get down to the floor and back up again quickly for other reasons, replace the Bicycle Crunch with vigorous marching on the spot.

Standing Twists

Goal: 20 seconds.

Muscles Worked: Obliques.

1 | Start in athletic-ready and spine-neutral position, legs shoulder-width apart and core engaged.

2 | Raise your arms (straight or bent), and rotate your shoulders to one side then the other as quickly as you can without compromising spine alignment or hip position (figs. 12.1 A–C).

Your knees and hips should remain facing forward and not twist with you. Stabilizing them, while twisting your upper body, provides additional core training in this week's routine.

● ● ●

12.1 A–C Standing Twists.

Opposite Knee to Elbow March

Goal: 20 seconds.

Muscles Worked:
Obliques, hip flexors (psoas).

This exercise could also be called a Standing Cross-Over Crunch.

1 | March on the spot lifting your knees high with hands at your head.

2 | As you lift a knee, try and touch your opposite elbow to your knee (fig. 12.2 A).

3 | Return to the center after each time, even if briefly, so that your back gets worked by repeatedly raising and lowering your torso (figs. 12.2 B–E).

Furious Bicycle Crunches

Goal: 20 seconds.

Perform Bicycle Crunches (p. 104) as quickly as you can for 20 seconds. Do not worry much about form.

Special Needs Modification
Bicycle Crunches: Slower with Feet Higher

Goal: 20 seconds.

Perform Bicycle Crunches but keep your feet higher in the air and reduce the scope of the movement. As long as you are using cross-body coordination and your core, you are fine.

●●●

12.2 A–E Opposite Knee to Elbow March.

CORE TRAINING

Weighted Side Bend on Ball

Goal: 24 reps (left and right equals one rep).

Muscles Worked: Transverse abdominis, obliques, deltoids.

1 | Sit on the ball in a spine-neutral position with even weight on both seat bones, legs about shoulder-width apart.

2 | Raise a weight or object overhead, maintaining spine neutrality by engaging your *abdominals* to prevent your shoulders from falling back (fig. 12.3 A).

3 | Curve your spine over to the side, shifting the overhead weight held in your raised arms, to the side. It should still remain aligned with your head—that is, do not shift your arms but bend your upper body. Your arms will go to the side on their own if they remained aligned holding the weight directly above your head, and you have correctly curved your spine and ribs (fig. 12.3 B).

12.3 A & B Weighted Side Bend on Ball.

● ● ●

4 | Go back and forth, pausing momentarily in the middle to realign your body each time you change direction.

The challenge in this exercise is to keep the ball stable under you while you create increasing pressure on one side. In addition to working your *obliques*, you will also be training hip stability with asymmetrical upper-body loading.

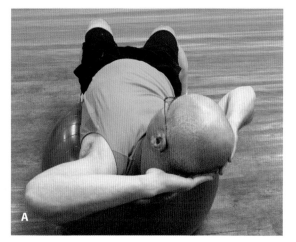

Ball Crunches with Curve

Goal: 10–12 each side.

Muscles Worked: Rectus abdominis, obliques, transverse abdominis.

1 | Perform a regular Ball Crunch (p. 87).

2 | At the top of the movement (you are in the crunch with *abdominals* working hard), curve your spine to one side as if you are trying to connect your armpit and hip bone on that side (fig. 12.4 A).

3 | Return to neutral and repeat on the other side (fig. 12.4 B & C).

The challenge will be to do this exercise while maintaining stability in your base so that the ball does not roll. You should only curve to the side as much as you can while keeping the ball under you stable.

●●●

12.4 A–C Ball Crunches with Curve.

12.5 A & B Ball Plank.

● ● ●

Ball Plank

Goal: To fatigue, 2 sets.

Muscles Worked: Transverse abdominis, obliques, shoulder stabilizers.

Perform a regular Plank (p. 95) but with your elbows on the ball instead of the floor. See how long you can hold it before you notice strength imbalances and find it difficult to control the ball. Stop when you reach that point or your back caves in.

The Ball Plank is, in one way, slightly more advanced than a regular Plank on the floor because of the introduction of the unstable surface of the ball. However, in other ways, the exercise is easier: the ball is soft on your elbows, and you are more on an incline, which reduces the pressure to your core. This exercise helps you to build deep-core strength, while continuing to work on your balance and symmetry.

1 | Start by standing on the floor a couple feet from the ball, and place your forearms on the ball (fig. 12.5 A).

2 | Stretch your body out and lift yourself up into a Plank position (figs. B–D).

3 | Make sure that you lift your seat only very slightly, tucking your tailbone down, and pulling your pubic bone toward your ribs.

4 | Use a mirror or a partner to verify that your hips are level, and that you have good alignment from heel through hip, to shoulder.

5 | Hold for as long as you can until you feel your back hollowing, then stop.

Note: You can also kneel on the floor in front of the ball to start if you find that you do not have the balance to shift from standing to stretching your weight over the ball.

12.5 C & D
Ball Plank.

● ● ●

If you are stronger on one side, you will notice a tendency for the ball to roll. Make yourself straight and strong by imagining that you are lengthening from the top of your head to your heels. You will be training your body to use straightening and lengthening as an automatic response to instability, instead of overcompensating for instability. This is very useful for riders, since many get into a pattern of being too busy with their bodies to fix problems instead of simply straightening, stabilizing, and centering.

Alternative Version
Plank with Legs on Ball

Another option for Ball Plank involves reversing which end of your body is destabilized by the ball. In this alternate version, your feet are on the ball, but your hands are on the solid floor. Each version destabilizes your body from a different end, working the core slightly differently. Some people find one version easier than the other

depending on whether they tend to be riders who rely on upper-body strength or lower-body gripping for support.

1 | Roll onto the ball on your stomach, placing your hands on the floor in front of you (figs. 12.6 A–C).

2 | Walk your body ahead of the ball by walking your hands forward until the ball is under your hips, legs, or feet (figs. 12.6 D & E).

3 | Align your body in a plank position and hold.

The proximity of the ball to your feet will be dictated by your shoulder strength, balance, and core strength. The more the ball is under your hips, the easier the exercise will be. The closer it is to your feet, the harder your core will have to work to keep your body weight from sagging by retaining a good, solid Plank position. Also, the closer the ball is to your feet, the more you are challenged to maintain straightness and symmetry without wobbling.

12.6 A–E
Plank with
Legs on Ball.

●●●

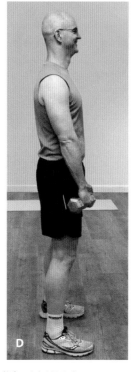

12.7 A–D Standing Deadlift with Weights.

● ● ●

STRENGTH & MUSCLE MEMORY

Standing Deadlift with Weights

Goal: 15–20 without pause.

Muscles Worked: *Gluteus maximus, hamstrings, lower back area, erector spinae.*

This exercise Standing Deadlift was first introduced in Week Two, but this week it picks up intensity and importance.

1 │ When doing the exercise, begin as described on p. 90, but now holding weights in your hands. Engage your *abdominals* and *erector spinae* by making your torso very straight as you tip forward from the hips. Allow your arms holding the weights to dangle downward. If you cannot keep a straight back due to the weight, reduce it (figs. 12.7 A & B).

2 │ Sit a little into your seat bones to engage your *gluteals* and *hamstrings*, in order to use your hip as a lever for lifting your back to the starting position (figs. 12.7 C & D).

It is very important to keep your back absolutely flat and not let it curve. Only tip as far forward as you can manage with a flat back. You may find the need to increase the bend on your knees and hips in order to do so. You should have a feeling of sitting down to lower your center of gravity. You should also maintain even pressure in both of your feet.

Special Needs Modification
Deadlift without Weight

Goal: 8–10 reps.

Follow the directions for the Standing Deadlift with Weights, tipping only as far forward as you can without compromising your back position, and not holding weights.

Advanced Variation
Deadlift on Balance Board or Object

Goal: To fatigue, 1 set.

Perform the Standing Deadlift with Weights exercise, standing on a balance board or another object that challenges your balance (figs. 12.8 A–D). A wobble board is *not* recommended since it is too volatile and "tippy." Examples of viable alternate options are a BOSU®, cushion, pool noodle, tennis balls, or a flake of hay (really!).

12.8 A–D Deadlift on Balance Board or Object.

● ● ●

Single Leg Forward Tip

Goal: 10–12 reps each side.

Muscles Worked: *Hip stabilizers, gluteus medius, hamstrings, erector spinae.*

1 | Stand with both legs together in an athletic-ready, spine-neutral stance. Arms at your sides (fig. 12.9 A).

2 | Lift one foot slightly off the floor so that all your weight is shifted onto the other foot (fig. 12.9 B).

3 | Maintaining a straight back with your arms at your sides, tip forward. Your free leg will rise up behind you. Keep your torso and free leg in straight alignment (fig. 12.9 C).

4 | Aim to obtain a perfect "T" position with your standing leg, hold it for 2 to 3 seconds, then return to the starting position (12.9 D).

As you tire, you may not be able to tip as far forward. Keep doing the exercise until you have reached the number required. Do all the reps for one side before switching legs.

12.9 A–D Single Leg Forward Tip.

Special Needs Modification
Single Leg Forward Tip with Balance Aid

Goal: 6–10 on each side.

Follow the directions for the Single Leg Forward Tip using one or both arms to touch or hold a wall or object for balance (fig. 12.10).

Advanced Variation
Single Leg Forward Tip Incorporating Arms and/or Weight

Perform the Single Leg Forward Tip. Once at the top of the movement, reach one or both of your arms forward in straight alignment with your body and leg, or as close to straight as you can get without compromising your body position or balance (fig. 12.11).

If two arms forward are too difficult, just do one at a time to start. If two arms are too easy, hold weights in one or both hands.

12.10 Single Leg Forward Tip with Balance Aid.

12.11 Single Leg Forward Tip Incorporating Arms and/or Weight.

DEEP STRETCHING

Stretch an area that is especially right for you; also focus on hip mobility by alternatively doing long stretches for the hip flexors and hip area, using the Hip Flexor to Ankle Stretch from the Standard Warm-Up and Hip Rotator Stretch from Week Four (see pp. 74 and 112).

STAMINA & COORDINATION

This week, aim to increase cardiovascular capacity with the warm-up rotation then move through the exercises with as few breaks as possible.

12.12 A & B Squats.

DISCIPLINE VARIATIONS

Intense

Supplement this week's exercises with two cardiovascular workouts. These can be done at the same time or later on. After warming up, do 15 to 20 minutes of speed intervals in the following repeated pattern:

1 | Spend 3 minutes increasing your speed (walking, jogging, indoor cycling—it does not matter). You should be breathing really hard by the end of the third minute.

2 | Follow this with 1 minute of continuous Squats (see below).

3 | End with 1 minute of walking to catch your breath, and repeat the cycle for 15 to 20 minutes.

Squats

Goal: As many as possible to fatigue.

Muscles Worked: Gluteus maximus, hamstrings, quadriceps.

1 | Start in athletic-ready, spine-neutral position with your legs slightly wider apart than usual (fig. 12.12 A).

2 | Keeping your head and chest upright, allow your back to fold considerably as you "sit down" (fig. 12.12 B).

3 | Ground your weight in your heels and start your lift back to neutral

from your *hamstrings* and *gluteals*—lift with your legs.

A common error made in this exercise is for the knees to be allowed to drive forward. This is especially common in those who need this exercise the most, because it is a body-compensating pattern where the body is not fully using the *hamstrings* and *gluteals* to support movement. It is a very bad mistake because it puts too much negative pressure on the knees. You should be able to see your toes past your kneecaps at all times, and have a feeling of sitting back behind you: it's a little as if you are squatting in the woods or over a toilet seat that you do not want to actually touch!

If you have difficulty with your knees driving forward too much, do the exercise against a box, hay bale, couch, or other low object that will block your knees from moving forward past your toes but still allows your upper body to come forward as your seat moves back and down.

Raised Seat
Build on last week's practice of "riding" a gymnastic jumping line ("Ride" Gymnastics Holding Water Glasses—p. 126) by increasing it to two different courses, with two different rhythms. Jump an imaginary pattern while maintaining core tone and balance. Also use a balance board this week if you did not do so last week (figs. 12.13 A & B).

Seated
Alternating Walk Patterns

Goal: 5–10 minutes.

Focus: Joint mobility.

1 | Alternate 1 minute of very long strides and swinging arms, with …

2 | 1 minute speed-walking steps (smaller, where you can really feel your hip and sacroiliac (SI) joint moving and arms pumping by your side) with …

3 | 1 minute of walking with alternative foot placement—for example, backward, sideways, on your heels, on your toes, and other ways (figs. 12.14 A–D).

12.14 A–D Alternating Walk Patterns.

● ● ●

Week Seven

Theme: Increasing core stamina, movement flow, and precision.

Equipment Needed: Small objects to place on floor as targets, hand weights, balance board or other balance tool.

WARM-UP

This week's warm-up incorporates an intensive, total body-core focus. Use the Standard Warm-Up Stretches (p. 67) but instead of flowing from one stretch to the next directly, insert a Core Training "pause" by doing a Plank (front or side, pp. 95 and 106) for 15 to 30 seconds in between each stretch.

WEEK SEVEN AT-A-GLANCE	
Warm-Up	Dynamic stretch routine with Plank exercises inserted for 15–30 seconds between stretches.
Core Training	Plank on Floor with Alternate Leg Raises; Spiderman Floor Slides.
Strength & Muscle Memory	Single Leg "Round the World" Reaches with Lateral Arm Raises; Deadlifts with Forward- Arm Reach; Squats on Balance Object with Arm Reach Forward.
Deep Stretching	Focus on lateral suppleness by spending extra time in Side Bends and Side-to-Side Lunges.
Stamina & Coordination	These aspects are incorporated into other sections this week.
Special Needs Modifications	Single Leg "Round the World" Holding Object for Balance; Squats on Balance Board Holding Object (or with Arms in Riding Position); Planks with Leg Raises while Inclined.
Advanced Variations	Deadlifts with Forward-Arm Reach—Adding Weight; Single Leg "Round the World" with Simultaneous Dynamic Lateral Raises.
Discipline: Intense	Mindfulness replaces cardio: Partner Mirroring Exercises for 3–5 minutes, 3 times in week.
Discipline: Raised Seat	Cardio work: Do 2, 15-minute intensity intervals.
Discipline: Seated	Cross-Body Multitasking with Larger Movements.
Notes	End routine with flowing Standard Warm-Up Stretches once or twice at the end (minus the Plank exercises).

CORE TRAINING

Plank on Floor with Alternate Leg Raises

Goal: Repeat to fatigue.

Muscles Worked: Transverse abdominis, obliques, shoulder stabilizers, triceps, gluteus maximus, hamstrings.

1 | Start by getting into a regular Plank position with either straight arms (as shown) or on your elbows, as needed (fig. 13.1 A).

2 | Once in a solid Plank position, raise one leg off the floor and hold for 3 to 5 seconds. Pay special attention to your pelvis and shoulder position. Your body should remain parallel to the floor and

13.1 A–E Plank on Floor with Alternate Leg Raises.

13.2 Plank with Leg Raises on Incline.

● ● ●

not twist just because a limb has been raised. Only raise your leg as high as you can while maintaining straight pelvis alignment. Do not allow your hip to fall on one side (fig. 13.1 B).

3 | Repeat this exercise alternating legs until fatigue.

Additional options include raising a bent leg (fig. 13.1 C) or raising each arm (figs. 13.1 D & E).

Special Needs Modification
Plank with Leg Raises on Incline

Modify the Plank exercise to do an inclined Plank on an object such as a bench, hay bale, or the arm of a couch. You can also be more conservative on the leg lift if you need to. Simply lifting one foot off the floor by a couple of millimeters will challenge your core in the way that this exercise is designed to do, but at a lesser intensity (fig. 13.2).

Going Deep

The Fit to Ride workout plan includes many exercises such as Plank with Leg Raises that are designed to stimulate the deep inner-core support muscles while also adding additional muscle movement or muscle combinations. This combines the benefits of an isometric exercise (where the effort is about holding the position) with an additional challenge to stability and coordination. You are asking your muscles to support your spine and keep it neutral despite the resistance from your own weight and added pressure of movement.

13.3 A–D
Spiderman
Floor Slides.

● ● ●

Spiderman Floor Slides

Goal: 2 sets of 60 seconds, or 20–30 "steps" (right and left equals one step).

Muscles Worked: Transverse abdominis, obliques, low back area, hip flexors (psoas), shoulder stabilizers.

1 │ Start in a regular Plank position, then bend one knee and slide the leg up toward your arms as if you were trying to climb a wall. Keep contact on the floor with your foot so that you slide your foot (figs. 13.3 A & B). In this picture, there are cloth potholders under the model's feet to assist sliding the feet. Performing this in your socks also works.

2 │ Return the leg to the starting position while sliding the other leg up (fig. 13.3 C).

3 │ Go back and forth "climbing" the imaginary wall until fatigue (fig. 13.3 D).

This exercise purposefully challenges you to maintain spine neutrality and alignment. You will wiggle your hips a fair bit, but focus on not allowing your spine to wiggle side to side. Visualize your spine as *rotating* rather than wiggling. Similarly, do not allow your hips to collapse toward the floor just because they are changing position. As you bend one knee and "crawl" that leg, you will need to keep your focus on your straight leg, and on the straight line between your head and the foot of the straight leg. Imagine as you "crawl" that you are lengthening the straight leg. The common temptation is to focus on the "crawling" leg that is moving, which often causes you to forget about your core and your position.

STRENGTH & MUSCLE MEMORY

Single Leg "Round the World" Reaches with Lateral Isometric Arm Raises

Goal: 4 "rounds."

Muscles Worked: *Gluteus medius and minimus, stabilizers in hip, knee, and ankles, quadriceps, deltoids.*

1 | Start by standing on one leg in a spine-neutral position.

2 | Raise your arms to shoulder height and keep them there throughout the exercise. Raising your arms will help you keep upright in your upper body, as well as straight. If your arms get tired through the exercise, you can lower them to riding position (figs. 13.4 A & B).

3 | Reach your foot toward objects like cones placed around you, keeping your core engaged. Reach in precise directions. Do not

●●●

13.4 A–D
Single Leg "Round the World" with Lateral Isometric Arm Raises.

13.5 A & B Single Leg "Round the World" Holding Balance Object.

● ● ●

allow imprecise swinging of your leg here and there. Go slowly so that you are working your hip-rotation-control muscles, instead of simply using momentum (figs. 13.4 C & D).

Use your core engagement to prevent your hip from poking out. If you lose your balance, reduce the bend in your knee and hold on to a stable object.

Special Needs Modification
Single Leg "Round the World" Holding Balance Object

You can do the Single Leg "Round the World" while touching or holding an object for balance (figs. 13.5 A & B). Take care not to transfer much of your weight to the object you are holding. Try and keep as much of your weight as squarely over your standing leg as possible.

Advanced Modification
Single Leg "Round the World" with Dynamic Lateral Arm Raises

Once you have mastered the Single Leg "Round the World" Reach, give your neuromuscular system a coordination challenge by combining the exercise with dynamic (moving) lateral arm raises (figs. 13.6 A–F). Use weights if you can or if you want to build increased shoulder strength. If your arms and shoulders fatigue before you are finished with the part of the exercise for your legs, stop using the weights but keep going. Adding simultaneous arm movement elevates heart rate and increases the coordination challenge.

13.6 A–F Single Leg "Round the World" with Dynamic Lateral Arm Raises.

● ● ●

Deadlifts with Forward-Arm Reach

Goal: 10–12 repetitions.

Muscles Worked: *Gluteus maximus, hamstrings, erector spinae, deltoids, lower trapezius.*

●●●
13.7 A–E Deadlifts with Forward-Arm Reach.

This exercise builds on last week's Deadlift, while adding difficulty for your back muscles, and for coordination.

1 | Begin a Deadlift without weights as described on p. 90 (fig. 13.7 A).

2 | As you reach the bottom of the movement (where your back is at its lowest), pause (fig. 13.7 B).

3 | Reach both arms forward. As you reach, you may feel a need to raise your back slightly depending on how well your lower back can cope with the added loading of your arm weight. Ideally, your goal is to have your arms pass your ears so that your arms and back are in perfect alignment (figs. 13.7 C & D).

4 | Pause with your arms in forward reach before returning them to the dangling position of the Deadlift, and finishing in the same athletic-ready stance you began (fig. 13.7 E).

13.8 A–E Deadlifts with Forward-Arm Reach— Adding Weight.

● ● ●

If you have a shoulder impingement, this exercise is not possible. However, you can still push the motion as far as you can until you feel your back and shoulder muscles engaging an extra amount.

Advanced Modification
Deadlifts with Forward-Arm Reach—Adding Weight

Perform the Deadlift with Forward-Arm Reach with weights in your hands (figs. 13.8 A–E).

Caution: Do not use too much weight. You might normally be able to lift higher weights than you use in this exercise; however, the bent-over position combined with lifting of weights creates an extreme lever at your lower back and requires full recruitment of your muscles from your lower back, all the way to your hands. Only use the amount of weight you can lift while keeping excellent form.

13.9 A & B Squats on Balance Object with Arm Reach Forward and Up.

● ● ●

Squats on Balance Object with Arm Reach Forward and Up

Goal: Repeat to fatigue.

Muscles Worked: *Gluteus maximus, hamstrings, erector spinae, deltoids, transverse abdominis, stabilizers in hip, knee, and ankles.*

1 │ Stand in athletic-ready and spine-neutral position on a balance object that destabilizes you side to side, not so much forward and back.

2 │ Perform a squat by folding increasingly at the hip and knee to sit your seat back behind you, and tip your torso forward. Only lower yourself as far as you can while keeping a straight back (fig. 13.9 A).

3 │ At the bottom of the movement when you have lowered yourself as far as you can go while maintaining a neutral spine, reach your arms forward and up. Ideally, you want your

arms to pass your ears or behind your ears so that they are in alignment with your torso (fig. 13.9 B).

4 │ After pausing a moment in this position (your back and shoulder muscles should really be feeling it), return your arms to neutral, and your body to the neutral starting position.

Special Needs Modification
Squats on Balance Board Holding Object

Perform the Balance Board Squats holding something for balance (fig. 13.10). Raising and lowering your body for the Squats exercise while on an unstable surface helps you improve your balance. Or, you can do them without the forward arm reach but with your arms held in a riding position.

13.10 Squats on Balance Board Holding Object.

● ● ●

DEEP STRETCHING

Focus on lateral suppleness by spending extra time in Side Bends (p. 69) and Side-to-Side Lunges for stretching the inner thigh (p. 75).

STAMINA & COORDINATION

These elements have been incorporated into other exercises this week.

DISCIPLINE VARIATIONS

Intense

You have spent a couple of weeks building cardiovascular capacity. This week you take a break from cardio to focus on mindfulness to improve reaction times. You will need a partner.

Partner Mirroring Exercises

Goal: 3–5 minutes, 3 times a week.

Focus: Be aware of your partner's movement and reaction times while maintaining balance.

1 | Stand in athletic ready and spine-neutral position facing a partner.

2 | Maintain spine neutrality as you adjust to different positions, taking turns mirroring one another (figs. 13.11 A & B). Move any limb or combination of limbs, change speed and tempo, or take steps or lunges in different directions. Your job is to stay accurate with as little lag time as possible as you mirror your partner's movement.

13.11 A & B Partner Mirroring Exercises.

● ● ●

Raised Seat

This week you swap out mindfulness and coordination exercises for cardiovascular-capacity training at least twice in the week. Pick any heart-elevating activity you enjoy: elliptical, running, cross-country skiing, speedwalking, cycling, indoor machines, hill running, or swimming. The mode of exercise does not matter. Do what fits in your schedule the best.

After a warm-up, do intensity intervals in a 1:1 or 2:1 ratio for 15 minutes. During the intense phase, give the activity 100 percent. During the recovery phase, slow right down to catch your breath so that you are ready to burst again for the next intense phase.

If you find that you tire toward the end of 15 minutes, intensity training may need to be a more regular feature of your training for a bit. If you find that 15 minutes, or the ratio, is not challenging you, change the ratio to 3:1 and go for 20 minutes. Whether you do the 15 minutes in a 2:1 ratio, or modify it up or down, your intense phase should mean that you feel you are getting out of breath.

Seated

This week you return to fine-tuning body coordination. You use the same type of exercise as in Week Five (p. 127), but make larger movements with your limbs to further challenge your core stability.

Cross-Body Multitasking with Larger Movements

Goal: 3–5 minutes, 3 times a week.

Focus: Balance and coordination with core integration.

● ● ●
13.12 A & B Cross-Body Multitasking with Larger Movements.

In this exercise you return to the athletic-ready and spine-neutral stance then incorporate larger limb movements to add an increased challenge to your maintenance of balance and core stability.

1 | Start in athletic-neutral stance and perform two separate activities with your arms, paying attention to your shoulder position.

2 | Shift your weight to one foot and elevate the challenge by moving the free leg and opposite arm in different patterns (figs. 13.12 A & B). See how large and different you can make the movements while still retaining a neutral-spine and a stable torso position.

Your torso should remain facing forward with minimal movement. To maintain stability, lower your shoulders, and make sure you are breathing from your diaphragm. If you lose your balance, stop, reset, and start again.

End your exercise routine with a round or two of the flowing Standard Warm-Up Stretches (p. 67) to loosen your joints and muscles.

Week Eight

WEEK EIGHT AT-A-GLANCE	
Warm-Up	Alternate jogging with one complete flow through Standard Warm-Ups, repeat 4–6 times.
Core Training	Ball Crunch with Weighted Single Arm Reach-Backs; Side Plank on Balance Object with Leg Lift; Superman on Balance Object.
Strength & Muscle Memory	Bridge with Alternate Leg Raise; Standing Leg Lift Moving into Forward Tip.
Deep Stretching	Focus on shoulder mobilization with Standard Warm-Up Shoulder Rotations, Wall-Assisted Pectoral Stretches from Week Three. Also do deep (hold longer) Side-to-Side Lunges and Hip Flexor to Ankle Stretch (Lunge and Press) for hip and ankle mobility.
Stamina & Coordination	Incorporated into warm-up and discipline-specific sections.
Special Needs Modifications	Bridge with Micro Foot Raise and Arms Out; Ball Crunch with Modified Reach Back; Side Leg Lift Moving into Forward Tip—Holding for Balance; Side Plank on Incline with Leg Lift; Superman on Floor.
Advanced Variations	Bridge with Feet on Ball; Weighted Ball Crunch with Reach-Backs; Side Plank on Balance Object with Weighted Lateral Arm Lift; Side Leg Lift into Forward Tip with Weighted Arm Reach; Superman with Added Limb Movement.
Discipline: Intense	Agility Drills: 2–3 times in week.
Discipline: Raised Seat	Ride a course with a pro (use TV or computer), 2–3 times for 5–10 minutes.
Discipline: Seated	Crazy Gait Drill variations.
Notes	Pay attention to rhythm and accuracy.

Theme: Increasing stability with asymmetrical challenges and agility.

Equipment Needed: Balance object, exercise mat, hand weights, objects for agility drill (the *Intense* regimen only).

WARM-UP

Keep your heart rate up while achieving maximum suppleness prior to your workout: Alternate between jogging and skipping on the spot for 30 seconds, with one complete flow-through of the Standard Warm-Up Stretches (p. 67). Repeat 4 to 6 times. (If jogging or skipping are not options, use brisk walking on the spot with arms pumping vigorously and knees lifted high.)

CORE TRAINING
Ball Crunches with Weighted Reach-Backs

Goal: 10–12 each arm.

Muscles Worked: Rectus abdominis, obliques, transverse abdominis, latissimus dorsi, triceps.

1 | Hold 5 to 8 pound weights in your hands and sit on the ball.

2 | Position yourself for the Ball Crunch as described on p. 87.

3 | Perform the Ball Crunches with Isometric Reaches as in Week Three Advanced Variation (p. 88), adding to the workload by holding the weights (fig. 14.1).

You may find that the addition of weight creates a significant workload to your core, and that you cannot reach your arm back as far as when you did the exercise without weights.

Special Needs Modification
Ball Crunches with Modified Reach-Back

Goal: 6–8 both sides.

For people with shoulder issues, you can perform the Ball Crunches with Weighted Reach-Back, but bend your elbows, or use no weight (figs. 14.2 A & B). You can also do the exercise beside an object you can touch or hold for balance, using one arm to steady yourself on the ball, and the other to do the reach-back.

14.1 Ball Crunches with Weighted Reach-Backs.

● ● ●

14.2 A & B Ball Crunches with Modified Reach-Back.

● ● ●

Advanced Variation

Ball Crunches with Weighted Reach-Backs and Arm Shifts

Goal: 12–15 each side.

This variation differs from the original (see p. 157) and is made more intensive by adding significantly more weight and arm movements.

1 | Perform Ball Crunch with Isometric Reaches (reaching back while in crunch on ball, see p. 88). Add a significant amount of weight.

2 | If you are thoroughly comfortable with reaching directly backward while holding the crunch position, add some variety and challenge by shifting your arm position out to the side, then back in again, before returning to the start position.

Side Plank on Balance Object with Leg Lift

Goal: 12–20 each side.

Muscles Worked: *Transverse abdominis, obliques, shoulder stabilizers, gluteus medius.*

This exercise is similar to the Side Plank with Aligned Leg Lift from Week Five (p. 122). However, instead of performing the exercise on a solid surface, use a *balance object* under your elbow (fig. 14.3). A BOSU®, balance board, balance cushion, soft cushion, or pool noodle are some ideas. If you are not quite ready to do the Side Plank on a balance-challenging object, you can add a little more of a challenge by doing the exercise on a slippery floor with a soft pad under your elbow—that will slip if you lose alignment. The goal is to maintain alignment despite some instability under your arm.

● ● ●

14.3 Side Plank on Balance Object with Leg Lift.

Special Needs Modification
Side Plank on Incline with Leg Lift

Goal: To fatigue, both sides.

Perform your Side Plank on Incline and include a slight leg lift, as on p. 123. Repeat until tired on one side. Then switch and do the same on the other side.

Advanced Variation
Side Plank on Balance Object with Weighted Arm Lift

Goal: To fatigue, each side.

Now that you have an established the Side Plank, it's time to add balance work and a weighted arm-raise to increase intensity, especially for the core, and to further challenge your stability.

1 | Lift yourself into a Side Plank with your arm or feet on a balance object.

2 | While holding the Plank, perform weighted lateral raises with your free arm (figs. 14.4 A).

3 | See if you can remain in the Side Plank long enough to do enough lateral lifts to tire your arm and shoulder. If you need to stop with the weight, continue doing weightless lateral arm raises to finish off your set.

4 | Repeat on the opposite side.

14.4 A & B Side Plank on Balance Object with Weighted Arm Lift.

● ● ●

For even more challenge once you have mastered this exercise, move your arm and the weight in different directions while maintaining alignment and core stability. If you are not quite ready to combine use of weight with a balance challenge, start by familiarizing yourself with using the weight on a firm base (fig. 14.4 B). Then transition to incorporating the balance challenge.

14.5 A & B Superman on Balance Object.

●●●

14.6 A–D Superman on Floor.

●●●

Superman on Balance Object

Goal: 20–30 or to fatigue.

Muscles Worked: Erector spinae, gluteus maximus, hamstrings, transverse abdominis.

1 | Lie face down on a balance object so that it is mostly under your hips and lower stomach (fig. 14.5 A).

2 | Engage your core then lift your upper body, arms, and legs as high as you can (fig. 14.5 B).

3 | Hold for 3 to 5 seconds before returning to neutral and repeating.

4 | Continue until you get tired.

Pay attention to the tendency of your body to subtly shift the workload to your stronger side. Do not let it. When the tendency becomes chronic, you have reached the fatigue point for your weaker side and it is time to stop.

Special Needs Modification
Superman on Floor

Goal: To fatigue.

Modify the Superman on Balance Object exercise by performing it on a solid surface that does not challenge your balance at the same time—the firm base gives better support. You can also modify the exercise by doing the upper and lower body lifts one at a time. Pay attention to symmetrical use of your body. Lift only as high as your weaker side will allow (figs. 14.6 A–D). Repeat until you feel fatigued in your lower back area.

Advanced Variation
Superman with Added Limb Movement

Increase the difficulty of Superman on Balance Object by adding opposite limb pair or an abduction/adduction movement when your limbs are raised to intensify the requirement for your core to stay engaged while you keep your balance. Once in the air, move your arms apart then back in again very slowly so that the overall time that your back is engaged to lift your limbs is about 6 to 8 seconds (figs. 14.7 A–G).

14.7 A–G Superman with Added Limb Movement.

● ● ●

STRENGTH & MUSCLE MEMORY

Bridge with Alternate Leg Raise

Goal: 10–12 each side.

Muscles Worked: Lower abdominals and back muscles, obliques, gluteus maximus, hamstrings.

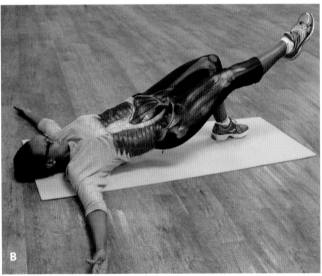

14.8 A & B Bridge with Alternate Leg Raise.

• • •

1 | Lie on the floor with knees bent as if you were going to do a Floor Crunch. Feet should be approximately shoulder-width apart, arms out to the sides as shown or down along your sides.

2 | Engage your core and lift your seat off the ground until there is a straight line from your knees to your shoulders (fig. 14.8 A).

3 | Hold for 3 to 5 seconds during which time you lift one foot off the floor while maintaining the alignment from your knees to shoulders, and across your hips (fig. 14.8 B).

4 | Return your foot to the ground; slowly lower your spine one vertebrae at a time to the floor until you are in your starting position.

5 | Repeat, lifting the other foot.

Do not allow your hips to fall down, or tilt. The goal of the exercise is to use your *obliques* and *gluteals* to maintain straight alignment in spite of the challenge added by lifting one foot off the floor.

Special Needs Modification
Bridge with Micro Foot Raise and Arms Out

Goal: 8–10 reps, both sides.

Perform the Bridge with Alternate Leg Raise exercise except keep your arms out to the side for better balance and minimize the leg lift (fig. 14.9). Even if you can maintain your position for a millisecond with a very tiny almost imperceptible lift of your foot, you are still training your core the right way for this exercise.

Advanced Variation
Bridge with Feet on Ball
Goal: 8–10 each side.

Perform the Bridge with Alternate Leg Raise exercise with your feet on an exercise ball (figs. 14.10 A–C). If you are very strong, you can try lifting one foot off the ball. You will have to roll the ball in a little with your remaining foot so that the other leg is in more central alignment with your torso.

Another challenging variation can be to do the Bridge exercise with your feet on the floor but your shoulders on a balance object. The ultimate challenge is to do the Bridge with your shoulders on a balance object and feet on the exercise ball!

●●●

14.10 A–C Bridge with Feet on Ball.

14.9 Bridge with Micro Foot Raise and Arms Out.

●●●

Standing Side Leg Lift Moving into Forward Tip

Goal: To fatigue, both sides.

Muscles Worked: *Hip stabilizers, gluteus medius and minimus, gluteus maximus, hamstrings, erector spinae.*

This exercise trains balance, hip stability, core strength, and coordination all at once.

1 | Stand in an athletic-ready and spine-neutral position: tailbone tucked down a little, and hips, knees, and ankles somewhat bent. This time, start with legs close together.

2 | Shift your weight to one foot (fig. 14.11 A).

3 | Raise the free leg to the side, as high as you can without compromising the upright posture of your body or the position of your foot parallel to the floor. You will not be able to raise your leg very high. You will feel your *gluteus medius* and *obliques* working hard to keep you aligned. If you can raise your leg very high, check your foot position; you are likely cheating by using your hip flexor and pointing your toe upward (fig. 14.11 B).

4 | Once your free leg is raised as high as it can go, rotate on your standing leg until you are in the tip-forward position as in Single Leg Forward Tip (p. 138) in Week Six, with your free leg straight out behind you. Your toe should be pointing downward to the floor, and you should now feel that your active muscles have switched to your *back, gluteus maximus,* and *hamstrings.* Extend your arms straight ahead (figs. 14.11 C–G).

● ● ●

14.11 A–G
Standing Side Leg Lift Moving into Forward Tip.

5 | Hold your balance for 3 to 5 seconds, then return to the start position and repeat.

6 | Repeat as many times as you can to fatigue, then switch sides and perform the exercise the same number of times as you did on the original side.

Note: Do this exercise slowly. Having control of your movement, being aware of your position, and precisely using the right muscle areas are the purposes of the exercise. Rushing robs you of the opportunity to improve balance and control.

14.12 A & B Side Leg Lift Moving into Forward Tip—Holding for Balance.

● ● ●

Special Needs Modification

Side Leg Lift Moving into Forward Tip—Holding for Balance

Goal: To fatigue, both sides.

Modify the Side Leg Lift Moving into Forward Tip by holding onto a solid object or wall for balance (figs. 14.12 A & B). The exercise is meant to improve your balance, but it is not cheating to hold onto something, or to make the movement smaller. You are still working the small stabilizing muscles in your joints, as well as proprioception and muscle control.

Advanced Variation

Side Leg Lift into Forward Tip with Weighted Arm Reach

Add a weight to the forward reach to intensify the balance challenge, as well as the workout for your back. When you have

14.13 A & B Side Leg Lift into Forward Tip with Weighted Arm Reach.

shifted to the tip-forward position, see if you can hold your balance while raising weights forward so that your arms are in alignment with your torso and leg (figs. 14.13 A & B). Start with raising a weight with one arm so your other arm is free to balance. Then add the second arm with the second weight. Another option is to raise the weights out to the sides.

DEEP STRETCHING

Focus on shoulder mobilization with extensive use of the Standard Warm-Up Shoulder Rotations and the Wall-Assisted Pectoral Stretch (pp. 67 and 100). Also focus on hip and ankle mobility by holding for longer the Side-to-Side Lunges and Hip Flexor to Ankle Stretch (Lunge and Press) from the Standard Warm-Up (pp. 74 & 75).

STAMINA & COORDINATION

This week, these elements have been incorporated into the warm-up and the Discipline Variations.

DISCIPLINE VARIATIONS

The speed work in this week's program is intended to train your proprioceptive awareness and ability to maintain a neutral and engaged core with joint suppleness while encountering unexpected or significant changes in your position. It is incredibly important to start out very slowly with all the speed work so that you gradually train

muscle memory and firing pattern. Be ridiculously slow. If you rush too quickly, you can risk exceeding your actual proprioception and ability to control movement. If you do this, you will train *compensatory patterns* instead of the precise body control with core engagement that you want.

Also, pay attention to the rhythm of your exercise. If you speed up and slow down, change your speed and rhythm precisely. Do not wander all over the map with random changing rhythms that you have not purposefully decided to use.

Intense

You will be doing at least two agility drills. You can be creative with this exercise and even look up additional options on YouTube. The basic idea is to set up an obstacle course that requires you to change your footwork patterns and use a lot of coordination. Run through your course at progressively faster speeds until you reach the maximum you can run the course safely and in full control of your body. See how many times you can repeat it at this speed inside 3 minutes.

Agility Drills

Goal: 2–3 times per week, 10 minutes.

Focus: Balance, coordination, and the ability to switch between tasks.

These add variety and improve your reaction times. Sample agility drill ideas:

14.14 A–C Agility Drills.

• • •

1 │ Set up items such as hula hoops or other objects that you step into, on, or over, in a pattern with spaces in between so that you have to speed up between stations then slow down to do the footwork.

2 │ You can incorporate your mounting block, hay bales, and pitchfork handles in a pattern to step on or over. One sample of a drill for foot coordination is shown here—walking and high-stepping over obstacles (figs. 14.14 A–C).

Raised Seat

Your goal this week is to improve timing response. The exercise is designed to simulate jumping a course in order to train endurance in your leg muscles with simultaneous core stability, joint softness, and responsiveness (eye-body coordination).

When you did a similar exercise earlier making up the course in your own mind (see p. 126), you had more time to prepare, and could create a next move based on your sense of balance. This week you *Shadow Jump*—that is, you follow *someone else's* ride. By doing this, you need to have much more control over your body's balance and continuously return to a neutral and ready position so that you can follow the course without getting left behind. By repeating the exercise for a longer time, you will challenge your ability to maintain focus and balance when you start to get tired.

Shadow Jumping

Goal: 20 minutes, 2–3 times in week.

1 | Position yourself in front of a television or other screen where you can watch a professional show-jumping competition. These can be live, recordings of the World Equestrian Games and the Olympics, or clips on YouTube, for example.

2 | Stand in your riding two-point position with a neutral spine and soft joints on two tennis balls or another balance object. "Ride" the course with the rider on the screen, and see if you can keep the same timing.

3 | Practice one or two rides (the same ones) until your timing is perfect, then see if you can follow random other selections from competition videos or YouTube, with better timing.

Note: To mimic a jump, drop your body *down*. Although jumping means that you go up on the horse, the biomechanical reality for your legs is that they *fold* in that moment as the horse and your stirrups rise up under you. To mimic this momentary demand for joint folding while keeping your balance, drop your body *down*.

Seated

This week's exercise works on your cardiovascular stamina as well as timing and ability to switch rhythm or gait. When your brain and body have trouble working together to make clean transitions in the type, rhythm,

or speed of the task you are performing generally, this has a negative impact on the application of this same ability in the saddle. When you train sharper response times on the ground, you will have much cleaner transitions in the saddle.

Most riders do not realize that transitions and gaits for your horse are not just a matter of you applying the right aid at the right time to start the motion. You also have to be suddenly on board and following the new motion with your body as well. Your horse can only transition into clear movements as cleanly and clearly as you can. Also, it is one thing to be able to switch tasks well, but it's an entirely different challenge to be able to do it over time, or in moments of higher physical demand.

Physically and mentally, a rider needs to have integrated core stability *and* trained her body to maintain softness in the upper body and suppleness in the hips at the same time as having a stable core. Otherwise, tensions and blockages in the body will stop the neuromuscular connections required for clear communication and switching tasks. The exercise is very challenging, but it's also fun!

Crazy Gaits Drill

Goal: 10–15 minutes, 2–3 times in week.

1 | Create a pattern using objects placed on the ground around your riding arena or other area. These objects should be about 20 steps apart.

2 | As you move between each object, change your "gait." Use *Crazy Gaits* like walking with high steps, running on your heels, doing sideways crossover steps, going backward, or any other footwork or body-locomotion pattern you can think of. However, don't make it up as you go along. Decide in advance what your pattern will be (or have someone else tell you). Part of the challenge will include remembering what is next while performing the gait you are in with focus and suppleness. You will need to mentally prepare a down- and an up- transition so that you clearly change at the change points.

14.15 Crazy Gaits Drill with Core Stability.

• • •

3 | Keep going with the same drill until you can do it cleanly, remembering all your tasks. When you can do a solid performance (and are likely out of breath), change it and do the second drill pattern until you can get it cleanly as well.

This exercise can be very physically gymnastic. Incorporate obstacles, cavalletti, or whatever you can think of that is safe. (It is also gymnastic for your brain!)

Crazy Gaits Drill with Core Stability

Goal: 2–3 times, 10 minutes.

1 | While doing your Crazy Gaits course, hold a bucket or large container (whatever your shoulders can manage) full of water over your head, or a bucket turned upside down with a ball sitting on it that could easily roll off (fig. 14.15).

2 | To keep the ball from rolling off or the water from spilling, you will need to maintain soft knee, ankle, and hip joints, an integrated and engaged core to stabilize your torso, and softness and relaxation in your upper body. Any rigidity, tension, or loss of postural alignment will cause you to misalign the bucket and lose the ball or water. If you have a shoulder injury or a biomechanical issue that prevents you from holding the bucket over your head, you can hold it up in front of you with the same effect; you can also hold eggs on spoons.

Week Nine

Theme: Putting it all together to challenge balance, stamina, and core integration.

Equipment Needed: Hand weights, exercise ball, exercise tubing, balance object.

Introduction: Congratulations! You have hung in there and accomplished a lot. The final workout will test your ability to integrate the elements you have been building for the previous weeks: body symmetry, core strength, core stability integrated with movement, proprioception, efficient movement patterns, balance, cross-body coordination, and stamina.

All of these elements have been blended together in different combinations each week, so that you were continuously working on them in different ways throughout. Sometimes they were a direct goal of a specific exercise. Other times they were an additional benefit, without being a specific objective.

WEEK NINE AT-A-GLANCE	
Warm-Up	Flow through the dynamic Standard Warm-Up Stretches 2–3 times continuously.
Core Training	Chainsaw Pulls with Overhead Reach; Weighted Standing Side Bend.
Strength & Muscle Memory	Combined Standing Leg Push with Opposite Arm Push; Forward Push on Balance Object—Single Arm Resistance; Side-to-Side Weighted Reach; Standing Reverse Fly.
Deep Stretching	Focus on shoulder mobilization with Standard Warm-Up Shoulder Rotations, Wall-Assisted Pectoral Stretches from Week Three. Also do deep (hold longer) Side-to-Side Lunges and Hip Flexor to Ankle Stretch (Lunge and Press) for hip and ankle mobility.
Stamina & Coordination	Incorporated into strength and muscle-memory section, and discipline-specific sections.
Special Needs Modifications	Simple Resistance Forward Push; Modified Chainsaw Pull Options; Modified Reverse Fly; Modified Side-to-Side Weighted Reach; Forward Push—Single Leg Resistance.
Advanced Variations	Combined Standing Leg and Arm Push on Balance Object; Side-to-Side Weighted Reach on Balance Object; Advanced Reverse Fly.
Discipline: Intense	Interval Speed Test.
Discipline: Raised Seat	Interval Speed Test.
Discipline: Seated	Introduce cardio intervals.
Notes	Consider cycling through the Fit to Ride Plan a second time, picking a different level of intensity or different discipline. You might be able to skip Weeks One and Two.

Do this week's exercises at the pace you need to. They can also be used as a fitness self-test to see how far you've come since you started. Remember that not everyone will rebalance her body at the same pace, or need to focus on the same areas.

WARM-UP

Just doing the Standard Warm-Up Stretches (p. 67) is fine this week. By now you should be completing them in just a few minutes.

CORE TRAINING

Chainsaw Pulls with Overhead Reach

Goal: 12–15 each side.

Muscles Worked: *Gluteus maximus, hamstrings, obliques, erector spinae, latissimus dorsi, rhomboids, deltoids, triceps, transverse abdominis.*

1 | Start in athletic-ready, spine-neutral stance, legs shoulder-width apart. Place a weight on the floor by the toes of one foot.

2 | Reach down and across your body to touch the weight on the floor, keeping your spine neutral even though you are rotating and bending (fig. 15.1 A). You will need to bend at the hips, knees, and ankles to perform a partial squat and use your *gluteals*

●●●
15.1 A–C Chainsaw Pulls with Overhead Reach.

to support your weight. Also pay attention to keeping your spine supported with good, straight back posture.

3 | Grasp the weight and sit a little more into your heels (and *gluteals*), engage your abs to support your waist area, and lift your torso back into upright position, holding the weight in your hand.

4 | Continue the lifting motion by raising the weight overhead. When your torso is about half way up, start to bend the elbow of the arm that is holding the weight. As you continue to lift your torso to upright position, pull the weight back in a motion similar to starting a chainsaw or lawnmower, and continue the arm movement until the weight is raised overhead (figs. 15.1 B & C).

5 | Follow the same movement path in reverse to lower the weight back to the floor in its starting position.

6 | Repeat all the reps on one side before shifting to the other.

It looks simple, but this is a complex exercise involving several planes of movement and several changing muscle combinations. Do not rush at the expense of form. Part of the value of the exercise is in training your body to stabilize through the *gluteals* and to maintain spine neutrality in spite of rotation, bend, and weight loading.

At first, do the exercise very slowly and perhaps with no weight at all. When you have the movement pattern mastered, you can add weight. The only limit to the amount of weight is the strength of your core and shoulders, and ability to maintain spine neutrality throughout the exercise.

Male riders may be able to lift more weight with the arms, but not without compromising other aspects of posture and ergonomic body usage. Do not get tempted to lift the maximum amount of weight. The goal is not to get the weight off the floor or to exercise your arm. Lifting too much weight can put negative strain on your lower back if your posture is not correct throughout the exercise.

Special Needs Modification
Modified Chainsaw Pull Options

Goal: 6–10 each side.

The Chainsaw Pull exercise is very challenging to the lower back and the shoulders. You can modify it in various ways for protection:

1 | Do the exercise with no weight.

2 | Bend your elbow.

3 | Don't raise your arm fully overhead.

4 | Hold a railing for balance.

Weighted Standing Side Bend

Goal: 12–15 each side.

Muscles Worked: *Obliques, gluteus medius, deltoids, transverse abdominis.*

The weighted standing side bend challenges your *obliques* and sense of alignment. Many riders with a natural "twist" in their posture unconsciously incorporate a twist into this exercise to manage the weight. Only use as much weight as you can manage while maintaining proper alignment.

●●●

15.2 A–E Weighted Standing Side Bend.

1 | Stand in an athletic-ready, spine-neutral position with legs shoulder-width apart, holding a weight in both hands in front of you (fig. 15.2 A).

2 | Lift the weight over your head and hold it there with symmetry in your arms and torso (fig. 15.2 B).

3 | Bend your knees slightly and drop your tailbone to ensure a neutral spine. Then, engage your core just before tipping over to the side, with the weight still directly over your head.

4 | Tip only as far as you can, while still being able to control the return (figs. 15.2 C & D).

5 | At the moment of return, press slightly more into the foot you are leaning over so that you can incorporate your grounding muscle memory into your torso lift. Finish the reps on one side before repeating on the other side (fig. 15.2 E).

If your arms and shoulders begin to fatigue, reduce the amount of weight. The goal is to challenge your *oblique* muscles, so use a weight that your shoulders and arms can sustain throughout the number of reps on both sides.

STRENGTH & MUSCLE MEMORY

Combined Standing Leg Push with Opposite Arm Push

Goal: 10–12 each side.

Muscles Worked: *Gluteus medius and minimus, adductor, hip abductors, deltoids, obliques, triceps.*

1 | Stand in an athletic-ready, spine-neutral position with legs shoulder-width apart. Stand with an exercise resistance tube or band under your feet, and either the same one or another one held between your two hands.

2 | Shift your weight to one side while maintaining an upright torso position, and lift your free leg to the side against the resistance of the tubing (fig. 15.3).

15.3 Combined Standing Leg Push with Opposite Arm Push.

● ● ●

3 | Push your opposite arm out to the side and upward, also against resistance from the tubing you are holding between your hands.

4 | Return to neutral position and repeat.

This exercise really challenges core integration, balance, and cross-body coordination. Use only the amount of resistance you can manage while controlling the whole movement. You should not feel that the resistance tubing pulls you back into your start position.

Also, start out by separating the two movements and doing them in sequence, but work your way toward doing them simultaneously. If you need to, first teach your body the movement pattern without resistance then introduce the resistance tubing or band.

It is a more effective use of your time to do all the repetitions for one limb pair before switching. By sticking to the same pair until you have completed the repetitions, you will build more stamina and you will avoid falling into a swinging back-and-forth motion.

Advanced Variation
Combined Standing Leg and Arm Push on Balance Object

Goal: 15–20 reps each side.

Introducing a balance challenge increases the difficulty level; only do it if you are very comfortable with the movement first. Perform the Combined Standing Leg Push with Opposite Arm Push while lightly challenging your balance by standing on a cushion or a flake of hay. If you can only do a few reps with this balance challenge, then simply finish the set with the standard version of the exercise.

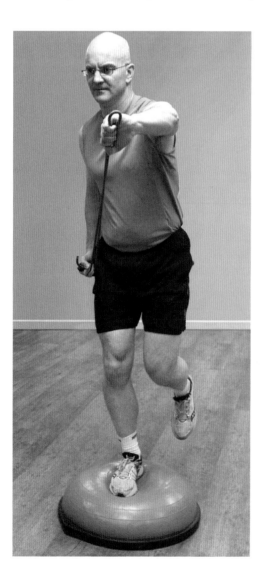

● ● ●

15.4 Combined Standing Leg and Arm Push on Balance Object.

STAMINA & CARDIO

Forward Push on Balance Object—Single Arm Resistance

Goal: Trains your body to use smaller stabilizing muscles accurately.

Muscles Worked: Stabilizers in hips, knees, and ankles, transverse abdominis, obliques, triceps, deltoids.

1 | Standing on a balance object in an athletic neutral stance, hold a resistance tube or band in both hands (fig. 15.5 A).

2 | Put one hand at your hip or slightly behind your hip. Push the other hand straight forward in front of your shoulder. You should be holding the resistance tubing or band so that you feel resistance as you push your arm outward (fig. 15.5 B).

3 | Return to neutral and repeat.

This exercise is simple from a weight-loading perspective. You will not be using the maximum amount of resistance that you could use in an isolated, pectoral-muscle-strength exercise. However, there are several complicated things going on that require your body to use smaller stabilizing muscles accurately: the coordination across your body of two different movements; the need to stay

15.5 A & B Forward Push on Balance Object—Single Arm Resistance.

● ● ●

balanced; and a need for your small shoulder-rotator muscles to work precisely while you experience a diagonal pull across a forward push.

If tension occurs in your legs, back, or shoulders as your body tries to stabilize itself, your balance will be thrown off. To do this exercise effectively, maintain softness in your *trapezius*, even though you need to engage your core and other shoulder and back muscles. If you have been training your previous weeks' exercises with accuracy, you should be ready for this one. If you find you

15.6 Forward Push—Single Leg Resistance.

• • •

are having difficulty combining the elements while remaining free of tension, break the exercise down into parts and teach your body the movement pattern without resistance first.

Special Needs Modification

Simple Resistance Forward Push

Goal: 8–10 each side.

Modify the Forward Push exercise by doing it without the additional challenge of standing on a balance object.

Advanced Variation

Forward Push—Single Leg Resistance

Goal: 15–20 reps.

Perform the Forward Push with the resistance tubing while standing on one leg (fig. 15.6). Your standing leg should be the same side as the hand at your hip. This will magnify the challenge to your hip stabilizers and core. You will need to have very high body awareness, a strong core, and the ability to maintain softness in your joints and *trapezius*.

Another option to increase difficulty is to increase the resistance-band's strength. If you can only do some reps with the balance challenge then finish the set with the standard version as above, which works as well.

Side-to-Side Weighted Reach

Goal: 10–12 each side.

Muscles Worked: *Gluteus medius and maximus, hamstrings, obliques, erector spinae, lower trapezius.*

This exercise involves coordination, proprioception, and good core strength.

1 | Start in an athletic-neutral position, then tip forward into a Deadlift (p. 90), holding light weights in your hands (figs. 15.7 A–D).

2 | With your back perfectly flat and your weight anchored in your *gluteals* and heels, reach one of your arms up so that it is parallel with your back. If you cannot keep your back flat while lifting the weight, reduce it (fig. 15.7 E).

3 | Curve to one side without rotating your torso. Your chest and stomach should remain pointing to the floor, with each shoulder the same distance from the floor. Reach your weight to the opposite side. It can help to imagine that there are two doors in front of you, one on each side, and that you are trying to reach the weight forward to touch the door handle. For example, if you are using the weight in the

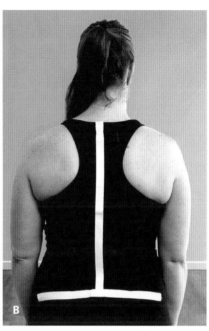

15.7 A–D Side-to-Side Weighted Reach.

● ● ●

  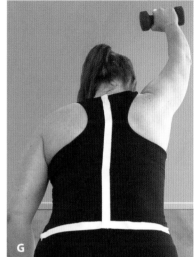

right hand, curve left and reach left (figs. 15.7 E & F).

4 | Return to the straight-backed position. Repeat, this time curving right, toward the *other* "door handle" (figs. G & H).

Curve your spine but do not rotate it or allow it to collapse. If you cannot lift your arm very high because of shoulder impingement, lift it as high as possible and imagine that it is extending straight out from your shoulder, and that this imaginary straight arm, or your shoulder itself, is reaching for the door knob.

15.7 E–H Side-to-Side Weighted Reach.

● ● ●

Special Needs Modification
Modified Side-to-Side Weighted Reach

Goal: 8 reps each side.

There are several ways you can reduce complexity or difficulty of this exercise:

1 | Tip less forward.

2 | Don't use weights.

3 | Hold a railing for balance.

4 | Don't lift your arm at all but still *imagine* a lifted arm so that you get the benefit of your back curving and your torso's reaching motion.

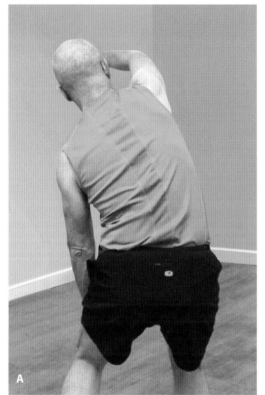

15.8 A & B Side-to-Side Weighted Reach on Balance Object.

●●●

Advanced Variation
Side-to-Side Weighted Reach on Balance Object

Goal: 15–20 reps each side.

This exercise greatly increases core engagement and skill for combining stability *and* softness in joints. You add a balance challenge to the standard exercise on pp. 179–180 by standing on a balance board or other balance tool (figs. 15.8 A & B). A wobble board or item with too high a degree of tip is not recommended since you need to be able to find and maintain a neutral-balanced position. If you can only do some reps with the balance challenge, and finish the set with the standard version of the exercise, that is fine.

Standing Reverse Fly

Goal: 12–15 reps.

Muscles Worked: *Gluteus maximus, hamstrings, erector spinae, deltoids, rhomboids, lower trapezius, transverse abdominis.*

Keeping alignment in the back and symmetry in the arm raises are the key goals here. Note how the shoulder-blades remain flat on the back and how shoulder-blade position is controlled by the position of the hands and arms. At the raised position, palms should be parallel to the floor. Most people need to think about keeping their elbows down in order to maintain palm and shoulder-blade position. The actual muscles targeted are quite small, so lighter weights are best.

1 | Stand in an athletic-neutral position, weights in your hands.

2 | Tip into a Deadlift position with your weight firmly anchored in your *gluteals* and heels.

15.9 A–C Standing Reverse Fly.

3 | Bend your elbows to a 45-degree angle and hold the weights so that your palms face each other (fig. 15.9 A).

4 | While maintaining the orientation of your arm and palms, lift your arms out to the side. Do not straighten them—keep the elbows frozen in their bend. You should feel your shoulder blades flat against your back and moving closer together (figs. 15.9 B & C).

The exercise is mainly for the *rhomboids* on your back, between your shoulder blades and spine. It is very important for you to use only the amount of weight you can manage while keeping correct arm alignment so that the movement properly isolates these muscles.

Special Needs Modification
Reverse Fly—Modified

Goal: 8–10 reps.

You can reduce shoulder strain, impingement pain, and the loading to your back and shoulders by:

1 | Tipping less forward.

2 | Not using weights.

3 | Using one arm at a time while holding a railing for balance.

4 | If you need to do a few repetitions and then rest before continuing to complete your set, that is also fine.

15.10 A–C
Reverse Fly—Advanced.

●●●

Advanced Variation
Reverse Fly—Advanced

Goal: 15–20 reps.

Add a balance challenge to the standard exercise by standing on a balance board or other balance tool (figs. 15.10 A–C). A wobble board or item with too high a degree of tip is not recommended since you need to be able to find and maintain a neutral-balanced position. If you can only do some reps with the balance challenge, and finish the set with the standard version of the exercise, that is an acceptable option.

DEEP STRETCHING

It's spine mobility week. Since you've worked so hard, spend time at the end of each workout focusing on back suppleness. The following exercises help your deep spine supporting muscles.

Relaxed Back Extension over Object

Muscles Worked: *Relaxing hip flexors, rectus abdominis, pectorals and small spine stabilizers (multifidae).*

1 | Sit on an exercise ball.

2 | Slowly lie back over it as you walk your feet away from the ball. Allow your arms to dangle on the sides (fig. 15.11).

3 | Stay in that position as long as you need to in order to fully relax. To get out of the stretch, simply reach one arm down to the ground and lower yourself off the ball to the side.

15.11 Relaxed Back Extension over Object.

15.12 Seated Assisted Side Bends.

Seated Assisted Side Bends

Muscles Worked: *Obliques, shoulder rotators.*

A helpful visual for this exercise is a mermaid, though if you are male, don't let this analogy put you off this exercise! It is common for men to be tight through the shoulders and upper back.

1 | Sit on the ground so that your feet are to one side. Hold a lead rope, yoga strap, or exercise tube in your hands.

2 | Reach both arms in the air over your head, and tip to the side that your legs are on so that you feel a stretch in your waist (fig. 15.12).

3 | Use the arm that is on the same side as your legs to pull on the strap, pulling your opposite arm more to the side than was naturally possible. The extra pull will increase the amount of stretch in your waist and *latissimus dorsi*. You may also feel good mobilization stretching in your shoulders.

Seated Twists

Muscles Worked: *Obliques.*

Seated Twists really help to mobilize your spine and rib cage by suppling your *obliques*. If the outer layer of *obliques* are more supple, your twisting motion will get into the deep spine stabilizers (*multifidae*), helping to restore the natural movement range to your spine. A locked spine is not good. A supple spine properly supported by core strength is supple, not locked.

1 | Sit cross-legged or with your legs straight in front of you.

2 | Twist to one side and grasp the floor with both hands to hold your torso in the twist (fig. 15.13 A).

3 | As you breathe and relax, slowly nudge your torso a little farther into the twist.

4 | Repeat in both directions (fig. 15.13 B).

15.13 A & B Seated Twists.

● ● ●

Hip Rotation on Floor

Muscles Worked: *Gluteus maximus, piriformis, IT Band, low back area.*

1 | Lie on your back on the floor as if you were about to do an *abdominal* crunch. Place your arms out to the sides in line with your shoulders.

2 | Tip your knees and legs to one side, and look to the opposite side with your head. If your legs can touch the floor, that is great. If not, you may need to prop an object under them so that you can relax into the stretch (fig. 15.14 A).

3 | Caution! In order to get out of the stretch and return to neutral before stretching in the other direction, start by curling up a little to protect your back. Then, bring your head and upper body over to the same side as your legs. Curl some more and roll onto your back to start again (15.14 B–D).

4 | Repeat in the other direction (15.14 E).

If you have benefited from the stretch, your small spine-supporting muscles such as the *multifidae* will be very relaxed. They are not designed to carry the weight of your legs, so swinging your legs over to the other side without taking measures to protect your back can cause negative strain.

15.14 A–E Hip Rotation on Floor.

●●●

DISCIPLINE VARIATIONS

The variations this week occur in the cardio-training segment. Otherwise, all disciplines share a common core of exercises.

Intense and Raised Seat

Add an interval speed test to your training routine.

Interval Speed Test

Goal: 3 times in week, 10 minutes total alternating intensity bursts (see below).

1 | Create a timed drill by setting two cones or objects approximately 10 running steps apart. Sprint back and forth for one minute between the cones. You will need to slow down, pay attention to ergonomically controlling your torso and joint position, and lower your center of gravity to change directions quickly while saving your joints to do so.

2 | Follow the one-minute sprint drill by doing as many crunches, push-ups, and squats as you can for one whole minute. Don't give up—keep going even if you have to slow down. Go back to sprinting.

3 | Alternate between the sprint drill, and an exercise, for a total of 10 minutes.

4 | Keep track of how many times you can do each.

Seated

Introduce Cardio Intervals

Goal: 3 times in week.

Boost your stamina by increasing your cardiovascular capacity and oxygen transfer (brain and muscles). Schedule three times this week when you can do 15 to 20 minutes of fast walking, jogging, or some combination of the two. Pick a specific route that takes you 20 to 25 minutes to walk at a business-like pace, but not so fast that you cannot still talk comfortably. Go out determined to make your time around this route shorter and shorter by increasing your speed each day.

Any combination of walking, speed walking, jogging, or running will do. Cycling also works. If you need to use indoor cardio equipment, you can modify this exercise by tracking your distance over 15 to 20 minutes and seeing if you can increase the distance covered each time. Your overall effort should feel like an "8" out of "10" *(for you!),* and include mini-recovery breaks (stay moving, but slow down) as needed.

Congratulations! And, Here's What's Next...

You have just completed a very intensive body corrective and reconditioning program. It's normal for you to have found that some of the exercises each week were not at your level. You may have even switched occasionally between the different exercise options: standard, modified for special needs, and advanced options, depending on how the exercise challenged your particular needs for symmetry and coordination.

To get even more out of the Fit to Ride program once you have finished Week Nine, you can go through the entire workout plan again, or pick out the areas that challenged you and combine them into a personalized workout for the next couple of weeks.

By completing this program, you have also learned about combining program elements into a single workout, or a weekly pattern that is complete (flexibility, core, strength, coordination, and stamina). You have learned many important points about posture, as well as how to combine exercises so that they are complementary. By keeping track of your progress you can see how much fitter you are!

If you are ready for something new (that is, you don't want to repeat this program since it is now easy for you), you can continue to create a similar training regimen by selecting from exercise options available to you for some of the components—for example, your run or favorite heart-pumping exercise class once or twice a week, plus your weekly yoga class and a daily habit of some of the stretches that you have learned.

Don't assume your new fitness level will stay with you; it has to be maintained. This means selecting activities for your week that help you maintain symmetrical body strength and core strength, cardiovascular stamina, flexibility, and coordination. You can maintain your fitness level by cobbling together an overall solution that works (use classes, books, videos, gym time), or you can contact me (equifitt.com) to design a next level program for you—or coach you online.

The rules of thumb for maintaining the fitness level you have fought to achieve these past nine weeks are:

1 | **Cardio:** Do for at least 15 to 20 minutes, two times a week. It can be as simple as speed walking and doesn't have to be the same activity. You can change it constantly. It's about getting your heart rate up in intervals for the right amount of time to maintain the level of oxygen transfer you need for effective riding. As a side benefit, you might find it motivating to know that heart-rate elevated

physical activity for at least 20 to 30 minutes significantly boosts brain-cell genesis and connectivity. This means you can think and focus better.

2 | **Core Training:** This can be done daily for a few minutes, or several times a week for a few minutes. It is better to train your core a little and often than to try and make up for lost time in big workouts. The smallest muscles supporting your spine and hips benefit the most from a few minutes of training, most days a week.

3 | **Flexibility:** Every day you are not stretching, you are losing flexibility. By now stretching should be part of your life—at least, the quick exercises from the Standard Warm-Up (see p. 67). Use them before major exercise, riding, or between activities.

If you have become more flexible through this program, you will have noticed that your body *wants* to stretch. You are now aware of when you feel "stuck." You can even pause your ride, get off the horse, stretch out the area that is gathering tension or stress, and get back on.

When you are frustrated or having difficulty with a movement with your horse, a little time-out for yourself can make a much more positive impact when you get back on, than the old habit of continuing to "hammer" on something that's just not working the way you want it to.

4 | **Coordination and Awareness:** Make it a part of your riding discipline to engage in an activity that you don't do all the time, at least a couple of times a month. This could be walking over varied terrain, going to the pool, trying your friend's fitness class—it doesn't matter. You don't have to be consistent about everything you do, especially if your goal is simply to put your body in an unfamiliar situation. Unfamiliar physical movements help your body stay sharp and keep an expanded physical vocabulary, as well as neural connections for range of movement.

Acknowledgments

As clichéd as it sounds, I would like to thank my parents for transferring to me their respective loves: horses and athletic fitness. When I was still a baby my mother made a papier-mâché rocking horse and sewed me a riding habit in the old style she remembered from the 1960s. I picked up my first set of weights when I was 14 because I wanted to be like my dad. I definitely owe them my gift for understanding biomechanics intuitively and my near-obsessive tendency to dream big, work hard, and pursue excellence in everything. My father, a former college teacher, meticulously reviewed my instructional design and exercise directions. This help is precious to me since he is in a wheelchair, living in negotiation with motor-neuron disease (PLS), which is merciless, relentless, and terminal.

My mother opened the door for me to live with horses, and to learn the value of helping horses and people do the most they can with what they have. While I like to think that what I have written fills an important gap in the literature available to riders, my mother's art in this book takes the work to a whole new level by demonstrating human anatomy that has never been illustrated before for riders. There were no similar drawings for my mother to copy. She often had to reconceptualize the muscles I wanted shown entirely in her head in order to complete the illustrations. We are both very grateful for digital technology since the drawings went through many revisions until they showed exactly what I wanted and were as accurate as we could make them. I am not sure I could have persuaded many other illustrators to collaborate on Skype between 10:00 p.m. and midnight (after my "day job") as she did. The time spent together has given us the kind of collaborative professional relationship that is rare, and made a way for closeness. I also believe it is the illustrations that really "make" this book.

I need to thank Trafalgar Square Books for embarking on this project with me. It takes a team to take a book from conception to accessibility.

I would like to thank other members of the book team as well: my friends, physiotherapist and photographer Carrie Smith, and exercise models Ifrah Ibrahim and Mike Van de Water. Mike trains for triathlons and runs marathons. He broke a sweat and had a few choice words for me from time to time. He would assure you that messing with neuromuscular connections and zoning in on structural support muscles is a hard enough workout for any gender, build, or fitness level.

Finally, I really need to honor the people who have invited me to work with them and the horses that have allowed me to be with, ride, and train them over the decades. I have learned some things from books, but most from the people and horses I train.

—

Index